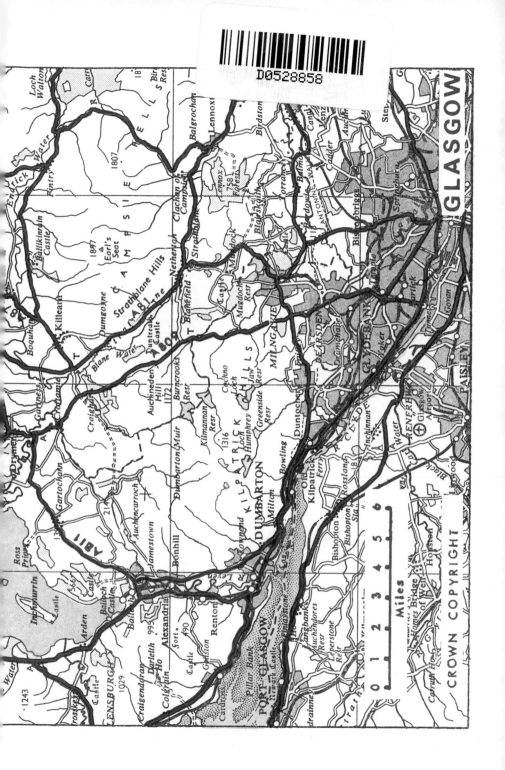

QUEEN ELIZABETH
FOREST PARK

Rob Roy and his wife, Helen MacGregor

FORESTRY COMMISSION GUIDE

QUEEN ELIZABETH FOREST PARK

Ben Lomond, Loch Ard and the Trossachs

Edited by
HERBERT L. EDLIN, BSc, DipFor
Forestry Commission

EDINBURGH
HER MAJESTY'S STATIONERY OFFICE
1973

Originally published as
The Queen Elizabeth Forest Park Guide
in 1954

SBN 11 490978 4

CONTENTS

ACKNOWLEDGEMENTS

THE verses heading the chapters on LochLomond and on Hill Walks are taken from *Sea Glimmer* (Maclellan, Glasgow, 1948), a collection of poems by the late William Jeffrey, and are reproduced by kind permission of Mrs. Jeffrey and the publishers. The verse heading the chapter on Mammals is from *The Praise of Ben Dorain* by the great Gaelic poet Duncan Ban MacIntyre, as translated by Hugh MacDiarmid in *The Golden Treasury of Scottish Poetry* (Macmillan, London, 1940); it is reproduced by permission of the translator and publishers. Assistance with the translation of the Gaelic place names has kindly been given by Mr. A. Nicholson, M.A. and Mr. J. M. Beaton. The cover picture is by Mr. James McNaught of Glasgow. The frontispiece and most of the chapter headings were drawn by Mr. C. W. Lennox Paterson, A.R.E., F.R.S.A., M.S.I.A. The drawings heading the chapters on Mammals and Loch Lomond are by Mrs. Vera Warrender. Those for the chapters on History, Forestry and Gaelic Place Names are by Mr. Colin Gibson, D.A. The following photographers kindly contributed the undernoted pictures: Mr. K. M. Andrew, plate 39; Mr. G. Douglas Bolton, plate 38; the Central Office of Information, plate 50; Fox Photos, plate 7; Mr. Andrew G. Gray, plate 21; Mr. G. Hughes, plate 28; Messrs. George Outram, plate 24; Mr. L. S. Paterson, plates 16, 48 and 49; *The Scotsman*, plate 36; Mr. G. Douglas Scott, plates 6 and 43; Mr. F. G. Sykes, plate 15; Mr. K. Taylor, plates 4, 62 and 66; Mr. B. S. Thompson, plates 51 to 58 inclusive; and Mr. T. Weir, plates 1, 12, 13, 14 and 30. Mr. John Marchington provided plates 59, 60 and 64; Mr. Roy A. Harris, plate 61; Mr. Eric Hosking, plate 63; and Mr. Geoffrey Kinns, plate 65. All the remaining photographs are by Herbert L. Edlin. The topographical maps, adapted by Mr. J. Watson, a Forestry Commission cartographical draughtsman, are based on the Ordnance Survey, by permission of the Controller of Her Majesty's Stationery Office. The geological sketch map and section are based on the work of the Geological Survey.

FOREWORD

BY THE SEVENTH EARL OF RADNOR, K.G., K.C.V.O.

CHAIRMAN OF THE FORESTRY COMMISSION, 1952-63

It is fitting that in commemoration of the Coronation of Her Majesty this most beautiful of the Forest Parks should be named "The Queen Elizabeth Forest Park". Her Majesty's gracious consent to her name being given to the Park is an indication of the keen interest that she and the Royal Family have always taken in country activities.

Of all the Forest Parks, this is likely to be visited by the greatest number of the public; for unlike the others it is situated within easy reach of the large populations of Edinburgh, Glasgow and the industrial districts of the central valley of Scotland. Moreover it includes part of the Trossachs which has for many years attracted visitors in large numbers from all parts of the world.

The Forestry Commission in 1928 acquired land in the neighbourhood of Loch Ard, and with later acquisitions have brought under national ownership no less than 42,000 acres extending from Loch Venachar and the headwaters of the Forth over the summit of Ben Lomond to the shores of Loch Lomond. The area marches with the main part of the beautiful Trossachs. Plantations covering an area of over 32,000 acres have been established, while 10,000 acres of lochs and mountains remain available for those who find joy and recreation in exploring the wild countryside.

While we rejoice in being able to offer these opportunities for enjoyment to our fellow countrymen and overseas visitors, let us not forget that it was owing to the inspired vision of the late Lord Robinson of Kielder Forest and Adelaide that forest parks were created in this country. His service to this country in organising the nations forestry from 1909 until his death in September, 1952, was a magnificent achievement. He was most sympathetic with the younger generations, a feature of his character to which his idea of creating forest parks bears witness, for in the woods and hills of the park he saw opportunities for the young in age and the young in heart to enjoy freedom in the wild beauty of nature.

Let all who use the Forest Parks remember this and make sure that they will do nothing to spoil this beauty for others, or cause trouble to farmers by disturbing livestock, leaving gates open or leaving litter about. Special care must be taken not to cause fires. A little carelessness in dropping an unextinguished match or cigarette-end may lead to acres of unsightly devastation, undo the painstaking work of the foresters, and cause great financial loss.

The compilation of the first version of this guide lay in the capable hands of Professor John Walton, who was associated with the Forests Parks from 1938 onwards. It gives me great pleasure to record the appreciation of the Commissioners for the way he brought to this task his intimate knowledge of the Loch Lomond and Trossachs countryside, which is now embodied in this magnificent Forest Park.

RADNOR

Och hey! for the splendour of tartans!
And hey for the dirk and the targe!
The race that was hard as the Spartans
Shall return again to the charge.

—Pittendrigh Macgillivray, *The Return: A Piper's Vaunting.*

HISTORY

By A. S. Macnair

PREHISTORY

There is little direct evidence of the prehistoric occupants of this region, except for the stone circle near the Aberfoyle Manse and a cup-and-ring marked rock near Corrie. The circle, which probably derives from the Bronze Age, was presumably of some ceremonial significance. The site was undoubtedly chosen for its seclusion and inaccessibility, situated in an amphitheatre of the hills on a low mound of dry ground surrounded by the swamps of the Pow and Park burns, with the nearby Doon and Tom-na-Glun Hills for a further retreat.

There are also reputed to be cup-and-ring markings near Gartmore on Corrie Farm and on a stone at Malling Farm, and there is evidence of several crannogs, or lake dwellings, in Loch Lomond, the best authenticated being off Strath Cashel point. There was also one in Loch Ard.

The Romans avoided coming into the area other than on punitive expeditions, although one of the earliest chains of defensive forts

1

may have been established immediately to the south, extending from Balmaha to Stirling along the south side of Flanders Moss. These forts are shown on the 6-inch Ordnance Survey maps as "keirs" at regular intervals. They may have been used after the Romans left, together with others on the north side of the Moss, which probably formed the frontier between the ancient Celtic provinces of Fortrenn on the north, and the somewhat nebulous Mannan to the south.

Flanders Moss, carrying as it does today, in its most remote parts, rank heather and sparse, but quite tall birch, was probably fired to prevent surprise by both the Romans and their successors. By the prevention of tree regeneration this gradually cleared the woods, leaving the land bare.

THE PERIOD 500–1000 A.D.

From about 500 A.D. the Scots Kingdom of Dalriada began to extend. Aedan, later to become the 49th king (A.D. 570–604) was known as Prince of Forth. He won the battle of Mannan in 581 and had a fort at Eperpuill (Aberfoyle; Doon Hill?). St. Berach of Termonberry (d. 595) had occasion to visit Aedan who was to arbitrate in a dispute the priest was having with an Irish "wizard". Aedan was so impressed with the saint that he granted him his fort at Eperpuill for his monastery "Cathair" in Alba. At the same time he may have moved to a more desirable location, quite possibly to Gartartan Castle (Little Arthur's enclosure) which may well take its name from Arthur, Aedan's son, who may also give his name to Glen Artney. An alternative is that the name is associated with the MacKeurtan or MacArtan family, well known in the district, though equally the family name may derive from the same Arthur.

The association of St. Berach with Aberfoyle is less tenuous in that the annual autumn hiring fair and market, held until about 1890, was known as *Feill Barachan* (St. Berach's Festival). Possibly it was at Aberfoyle that the saint healed two lepers, the only miracles with which he is credited during his brief stay in Scotland.

THE PERIOD 1000–1425 A.D.

The political history of the area, except in the more remote highland parts, was dominated by the feudal barons. The Menteith, Comyn and Stewart Earls of Menteith for the greater part of the area, and in the south and west the Earls of Lennox and their subordinates the Drummonds, descended from Maurice the Hungarian, Thane Seneschal of Lennox in 1066, the Buchanans of Auchmar, and the MacFarlanes.

Menteith in its prime, originally based on the Rednock-Ruskie area, included all of what is now Perthshire in the Forth drainage

2

area, except Balquhidder and Strathyre which belonged to Strathearn; including the present parishes of Aberfoyle, Callander, Kilmadock, Dunblane and Lecropt, part of Logie, Kincardine, Port of Menteith and part of Kippen, now in Stirlingshire. The centre of the earldom was latterly Doune Castle, built after 1390 on the site of an earlier structure. There is a record of an Earl of Menteith sending a gift of two slaves to the Abbot of Inch Affray.

The original earls had the name Menteith, but as the title was heritable through the female line, the family name changed by marriage first to Comyn and then to Stewart. It was a Walter Comyn who endowed the St. Augustine monastery on Inchmahome in 1238, but it was a Stewart earl who became Duke of Albany in 1398.

It is quite possible that the country was more peaceful before 1400 than it was during the succeeding 50 years, although the barons often fought amongst themselves. After the killing of Gilbert Drummond in 1330, there was a blood feud between the Menteith faction and the Drummonds which culminated in the clan battle at Tarr, in which three Menteith nobles were killed. This was only settled by the intervention of the King in 1360.

In 1425 Murdoch, Duke of Albany, Earl of Fife and Earl of Menteith, who had succeeded his father as Regent of Scotland, while James I was captive for many years in England, having failed to gather the necessary ransom for the King's release, lost his head at Stirling in company with his sons. All estates and titles were forfeit. The structure on the island Dun Dochil, or Duke Murdo's Island, in Loch Ard is reputed to have been built by Duke Murdoch as a hideaway in anticipation of the royal displeasure. At the same time, in James' general purge, Malise Graham, Earl of Strathearn, merely lost his land and titles.

Until their power was broken, the Earls of Menteith, Strathearn and Lennox were no doubt strong enough to protect their lands from the depredations of raiders from the north. After 1425, the Highland marches were no longer so adequately protected, and no doubt this was one reason for the inclusion of 42 men-at-arms in the Duchray feu charter of 1492.

THE PERIOD 1425 – 1680

The next 250 years of history in this district was determined by the Grahame Earldom of Menteith, the Stewartry of Menteith, and to the south the ending of the Earldom of Lennox and the gradual ascendency of the Grahams (Montrose) over the Drummonds and Buchanans.

In 1427, two years after the abrupt demise of the Duke of Albany, James I reconstituted the Earldom of Menteith by a grant of land

3

and the title to Malise Grahame. The earldom was insignificant compared with its predecessor and to Malise Grahame's own previous earldom of Strathearn. It comprised only what is now the parish of Aberfoyle and the western part of the Port parish, and was no doubt the major factor determining their existing boundaries and thereby the present county boundary between Perthshire and Stirlingshire.

The rest of the lands in Menteith, including Duchray and Glenfinlas, remained with the crown, at least temporarily, as the Stewartry of Menteith. The charter to Malise Grahame listed all the lands by name, nearly all recognisable today (see list at end of chapter).

The centre of the reconstituted earldom was the Port of Menteith, and shortly after its inception the building of the castle was started on the small island in the Lake of Menteith adjacent to Inchmahome, which takes its name Talla (the hall) from the Castle. Two structures on the island, a round tower and a large rectangular structure, were probably built by the 7th Earl in the 17th century who had an aggrandisement phase. He was even foolish enough to lend money to Charles II.

James' object was to break the power of the feudal barons and in this case there is no doubt he succeeded. The area of the reconstituted Earldom of Menteith is poor agriculturally, and succeeding earls were always in financial difficulties trying to keep up appearances. There are numerous records of transactions, charters of land to relations mainly, and subsequent redemptions. In 1512, the area of what is now the centre of the village, "Craiganess and Craiguchty", went to John Colquhoun of Luss. In 1512, Lord Kilpont (Master of Menteith) redeemed from his great uncle Walter Grahame, for 500 marks (£27 sterling) the lands of Lochton (Achray), Inchre, Mylntoun and Kirktoun, Bofrieshlie, Bonante, Dounans, Baleith and Gartlamonbege (Gartloaning) and other properties. The above-mentioned Walter Grahame and his heirs owned much of the area of Aberfoyle parish at various times, and as late as 1625 Walter's great grandson, Thomas, renounced Glassfore (Glassert), Discheratyre (Dasher) and Blairuskinmore, in favour of the 7th Earl. It was this same earl who acquired the Barony of Drummond (Drymen-d) in 1631 from John (Drummond), Earl of Perth, finally severing the connection of the Drummonds with the area.

It was, however, a brief resurgence and Earl William, the 8th and last (1667–1694), sold all the lands of the Earldom of Menteith to the Marquis of Montrose (Graham) in 1680. He died in near poverty and without heirs. Although both the Grahames of Gartmore and Rednock were originally cadet branches of the Menteith family,

4

the connection had all but died out and left only debts to inherit. The Gartmore lands appear to have always been independent of the reconstituted earldom, although they may have originally formed part of the Stewartry of Menteith. Robert, the first laird, younger son of William the 3rd Earl Menteith, bought the property in 1547 from Alexander Macauly, and further land from Walter Macauly in 1554. The first of the Rednock Grahames was George, second son of John the 4th Earl.

The Stewartry of Menteith was gradually split up under various ownerships, although some areas were retained by the Crown for a prolonged period. In particular Glenfinlas was "afforested" by James II in 1454, and at least at the beginning of the 20th century it was to some extent still a royal forest; although there is no record of it having been used by any monarch for hunting after the Union of the Crowns (1603). Before that, however, it was used quite frequently. A Hunt Hall was built in 1458 and there are references to James IV hunting in Menteith in 1492 and 1496. The same James enjoyed a different form of hunting in 1489, when after having marched overnight from Dunblane, he surprised the Earl of Lennox, who was encamped at the Moss of Talla, and chased him as far as Gartalunane. In 1528 James Stewart (Captain of Doune Castle) was appointed Steward of Menteith and by 1612 James Stewart, Earl of Moray, was referred to as Heritable Forester of Glenfinglas, when he lodged a complaint against Alexander Grahame of Craiguchtie for poaching.

Duchray was also afforested for a period in the 15th century, though it appears to have been let to various individuals. In 1456 and later, the laird of Buchanan paid rents of Duchray and Drummond from, or for, iron made in these districts. In 1467 Donald Neyssoune was appointed forester and there is reference to repairs to a hunting lodge in 1469. In 1461 the "fermes" (rents) of Duchray went to the King, but from 1463 until at least 1480, the rents appear to have been assigned to Elizabeth Dunbar, lately Countess of Moray, wife of Sir John Colquhoun of Luss, a favourite of James III.

The charter for Duchray was granted in 1492 to Walter MacFarlane (possibly of Gartartan?). The feu conditions included his having to build a castle by 1514 and to maintain 42 men-at-arms for the service of the Crown. These men saw service on several occasions. In 1643 they were used by the Earl of Menteith, on the orders of General Monk, to cut down the woods of Milton and Glassart to stop them harbouring "loose, idle and desperate persons", but ten years later they were out in Glencairn's rebellion (1653), and were no doubt involved in the skirmishes at Glenny

5

and the Pass of Aberfoyle, following which the parish was laid waste by the English army. It seems quite possible that in later years, known as the Black Watch (Graham tartan?) and the "Forty-twa", they formed the nucleus of the 42nd of Foot Royal Highland Regiment (Black Watch), raised at Aberfeldy in 1739.

Although the original charter for Duchray was granted to a MacFarlane by the early 16th century, it had passed to Grahams, of a cadet line of Inchbrakie, possibly by marriage, as later did the Rednock lands of the Menteith Grahames.

The weakness of the landowners to the south of the Highland line made depredations from the north inevitable. In 1540 or 1544, a party of Stewarts of Appin, returning from an expedition into Stirlingshire, are reputed to have called in at the Port of Menteith and discovered a wedding repast laid out awaiting the return of the guests from church. Needless to say, when the wedding party returned, they found everything gone. The Earl of Menteith, who was one of the party, set out in pursuit. The raiders, no doubt encumbered by their booty, were overtaken above Glenny, but were too strong for the attackers and the unfortunate earl was killed by Donald nan Ord near Toberanreal, the Tchyepers Well. There are instances of other raids, and of course the MacGregors, who had been forced out of Breadalbane by the Campbells, moved into the no-man's-lands of Balquhidder and Glengyle over which, even in their prime, Strathearn and Menteith had probably little practical control. These lands, until the end of the 18th century, appear to have belonged to whoever could occupy and hold them by force of arms (sorning), although coming under the nominal control of Atholl.

In 1566, Archibald Edmonstone of Rednock was one of the tenants of the Stewartry who complained to the King against the action of the Steward in collecting rents as their lands had been "spoiled and wasted" by Clan Gregor. Previously, in 1553, it is recorded that the MacGregors had stolen 40 cows from Earl Alexander and his son.

The unsettled state of the area is evinced by the order from Holyrood in 1585 when "The King and his council, being informed that his good and peaceable subjects inhabiting the countries of the Lennox, Menteith, Stirlingshire and Strathearn are heavily oppressed by reif (plunder), stouth (theft) and sorning (squatting by force of arms without payment of rent) and other crimes daily and nightly"—twenty-eight lairds were asked to appear at Stirling. The MacFarlanes did not attend, being no doubt implicated in the activities described.

The battle of Glen Fruin took place in 1603, when the MacGregors, aided by the MacFarlanes, overwhelmed their traditional enemies the Colquhouns, and were outlawed as a result. The MacGregors in particular must have continued to make a nuisance of themselves as there was a further proclamation in 1611 ordering "all betwixt 16 and 60 years within the Shire of Dunbarton, Stewartry of Menteith and six parishes of Lennox" to meet at the head of Loch Lomond for the purpose of carrying boats to Loch Katrine. The success of this expedition, if it even took place, must have been limited. Two years later Finlay Kyill McKeith in Brenachyle was fined for aiding Clan Gregor.

THE SOCIAL BACKGROUND: 1425–1680

This state of affairs existed to some extent due to political forces, but was also due to economic and social pressures. For the available land there was a considerable population in the highland areas, and in addition the traditional mode of living was pastoral and hunting, not the cultivation of land. Livestock was wealth and the fat cattle of the lowlands represented a considerable temptation to a country full of "idle people accustomed to bearing arms". Over several centuries, the traditional manner of hunting red deer was by the "Tynchel" (*tienne seilg*) where the whole population of an area gathered and herded the deer into the "Elrig" (*allar rebb*) stockade after which they could be killed at leisure. That this method was effective is demonstrated by the comment by the minister of Aberfoyle in 1812, that only in hard winters were red deer to be found as far south as Glenfinglas and exceptionally Craig Vat (Mhadaih)—Slate Quarries. The same man commented on the lack of salmon in the Forth due to the floating of peat. This would not have pleased the monks of Inchmahome, who, in 1528, were granted rights to "fishing on the lowis (lochs) and stankis (pools) of Lugnoch (Lubnaig), Bannachar (Venachar) and Gude (Goodie).

During this period the ownership of the Glen Dubh (probably Buchanan) is not clear, but there is no doubt that in common with most of the land between Loch Lomond and Gartmore, it was occupied and at least partly owned by MacFarlanes, Macnairs, and latterly MacGregors. In 1457 there is reference to "McNayr inhabitants terras" Duchray, and later Humphrey MacFarlane of Brackearn (Bruach Chaoruinn) was a son of Andrew, 4th Chief (1547–1612). Gartartan was the home of another cadet branch of the clan, from the 15th century until after 1724 when it was occupied by Andrew MacFarlane. In 1630, Duncan Moir MacFarlane Brackearne was one of the heritors of the parish of Buchanan, whom the first minister raised a complaint against, concerning the ruinous condition of the parish church in Inch Cailleach. In 1650

7

Buchanan of Arnprior had charter of the land from John Macnair but sold out soon afterwards to Duncan MacFarlane, after having trouble with a band of outlaws under "Captain McTormed" who occupied his property. Buchanan is reputed to have disposed of them by setting fire to the tavern at Chapelarroch.

This tavern, in the next century, was the scene of one of Rob Roy's better authenticated escapades; when he captured Graham of Killearn, the Duke's factor, together with £300 of rent money. Rob Roy was, for a period, owner of Craigrostan, the land from Ardess to the north as far as the county boundary, by a charter of 1706 from McGregor of Kilmannan, the clan chief, who had previously acquired it from Colquhoun of Luss in 1693. Rob Roy lost these lands to the Duke of Montrose shortly afterwards, following legal action for alleged debt; it is doubtful that the land was legally wadset. He was outlawed for the first time as a result of the same proceedings.

Another, apocryphal, story, of possibly good foundation, records the grant by the Earl of Menteith of the lands of Bruchorn together with his ward the orphaned daughter of Grahame of Dounance (Aberfoyle) for a wife to Robert Grahame, the younger son of Glaschoil on Loch Katrine. This arose in recompense for the earl having instigated the death of Malise Graham, his wife's cousin and Robert's father, in a fit of alcoholic jealousy after a party at Talla many years before. If true, it must have been the 7th Earl, who had probably bought the land from Duncan MacFarlane. As a result, this land would also have passed to the Duke of Montrose in 1680 with the rest of the Earldom of Menteith. It cannot, however, have included all the lands as in 1691 Isabella Graham, relict of John McGregor of Brachern and then spouse of Malise Graham in Dunaverig, disposed of East and West Brachern and Stron McNair to her nephew Alexander Graham. Transactions in the area are complicated at this period by the fact that the name McGregor was proscribed; all McGregors were obliged to take the name Graham.

THE PERIOD 1680–1800

From 1680 the Duke of Montrose owned the whole Forest Park area with the exception of Duchray, including Corriegrennan, owned by Graham of Duchray and Rednock; and Craigrostan and parts of Glen Dubh, though these latter were "acquired" in the early part of the 18th century.

In the first, 1715, Jacobite Rebellion, in which the MacGregors played an active part, the bridge of Aberfoyle was destroyed and Duchray Castle burned. The bridge was still not repaired in 1724 and it was 100 years before Duchray Castle was reoccupied. The

Plate 1. Water ski-ing on Loch Lomond, seen from Rowardennan beach.

Plate 2. Loch Lomond at Balmaha; the broad lower reaches, with the islands of Clairinch in centre and Inchcailloch close by on right. Note the water ski-er.

Plate 3. Waiting for the ferry from Balmaha to the Nature Conservancy's Reserve on Inchcailloch.

Plate 4. Looking north-west up Loch Lomond from Balmaha, over Inchfad towards the snow-clad peaks around Arrochar.

Plate 5. The anchorage at Balmaha, sheltered by the pines and oaks of Inchcailloch.

Plate 6.   Ben Lomond's summit.   The north face in winter.

Plate 7.   Sunset over the northern reaches of Loch Lomond; looking from Rowchoish towards
Ben Vorlich, left and far Ben Lui.

Plate 8.　The beach at Rowardennan, Loch Lomond.

Plate 9.   The ruins of the garrison barracks at Inversnaid, used today as a sheepfold.

Plate 10. Loch Lomond at Inversnaid, looking towards Ben Vorlich.

Plate 11. The falls at Inversnaid.

county, however, was becoming more developed under the protection of the "new built barrack of Inversnaat" which accommodated 100 men. Between the two Jacobite risings the military road was built to Inversnaid and also Gartmore bridge. In 1732 the Aberfoyle manse was built and in 1744, the old church. Some years earlier (1727) John Blair was appointed catechist in the heads of Drymen and Buchanan parishes, an area which had until then been predominantly Catholic. This was probably the first Presbyterian ministry they had known. In 1768, Wester Duchray (Corriegrennan) was leased by a Blair. The Blair family, until recently, were well known in the area as farmers and hotel proprietors and may have descended from Donald Blair, alias "Kittoche of Aberfoyle", witness to a McGregor affray at Leny in 1626. It also appears that some local schools were started during the period.

The first action of the second, 1745, Jacobite Rebellion, was the seizure of Inversnaid Barracks by the MacGregors. But for a period Rob Roy worked at least ostensibly on the side of the law by organising the Highland Watch to prevent raiding from the north on Lennox and Menteith. By this means he was more or less given legal authority to levy blackmail; those that did not pay their dues were liable to lose their cattle; an extortion racket with legal backing! This Watch was later carried out by his nephew Ghlun Dhu MacGregor of Glengyle who charged £4 for every £100 of rent.

The last recorded MacGregor outrage was perpetrated by the sons of Rob Roy whose character may well have been warped by their disturbed youth. On the evening of 8th December 1750, Jean Key, a widow of six weeks' standing, though only nineteen years of age, and portioner of Edenbellie, Balfron, was carried off by James and Robert (Robin Oig) assisted by Ronald and Duncan MacGregor. Two days later she was forcibly married at Rowardennan to Robin, who planned thereby to make his fortune. The plan would probably have succeeded even fifty years before, but the law eventually forced her release and the culprits were brought to justice, although the poor terrorised girl died of smallpox in Glasgow before the trial. James, probably the instigator, escaped to France from Edinburgh Castle while his sentence was being considered. Duncan was acquitted, but Robin, who was already wanted for a Balquhidder murder committed at the tender age of 15 years, was hung in 1754, after capture whilst attending a fair at Gartmore.

THE SOCIAL BACKGROUND: 1680–1745

Although the economy was largely pastoral in the Highlands, on the fringes, in addition to an increase in cultivation over the centuries, industry was not entirely lacking. In the 15th century there was an iron trade at Aberfoyle, attracted no doubt by the plentiful supply of birch charcoal, although iron ore would have to be brought in, as it was from Holland 300 years later when Alexander Grahame of Duchray reports an iron works three miles north of Aberfoyle Church, probably at Achray. There are slag iron sites at Loch Katrine and Loch Lomond side. It is also likely that the "Hewch" from which the Earl of Menteith was ordered to supply slates from Stirling Castle in 1574, was situated at Aberfoyle, although probably not used extensively until the 19th century. It was noted for "excellent blew sclait" in 1724. Alexander Grahame of Duchray, who commented on the slate, also worked the lime above Dounans quite extensively, and quarrying continued, latterly on a commercial basis by Sorley and MacFarlane until virtually worked out by 1850. Barytes was quarried on the ridge between Clashmore and Gartmore at least from 1882–87, reputedly as much for its lead content as for barium.

Flax was grown quite extensively as a cash crop and there were a number of lint mills in the district, including one at the Milton. This industry, which involved steeping the stems in water until the fibres separated, was disliked by the fishing interests. A pond by the road out of Aberfoyle to the east, served this purpose, giving its name to the river ford nearby, Ath-len-an (Alinan), or the linen ford.

More numerous were the corn mills; mills throughout Scotland were a landowners' monopoly, as in 1285 querns (hand mills) had been prohibited by law; and there were plenty built in this area. The Milton is mentioned as belonging to the Earl of Menteith in 1485 and the remaining building has a stone engraved "E.W.M. 1667" commemorating the last Earl, William of Menteith. This mill functioned until 1914 and the Mill of Chon only closed in the mid-19th century. Other mills were situated at Ledard, Achray, Loch Drunkie, Malling, Inchrie and Stronachan, and in addition, although there is no direct record, there must have been another mill at Cuil Muilinn, 200 yards upstream from Bruach Chaoruinn. Although it may not have been a very big mill, for there to have been a mill at all gives some indication of the extent of population and cultivation in Glen Dubh.

In 1759 there were ninety-one people, in sixteen families, living in the glen between Comer and Stucabhuich, two families each, and Coryghrenen, one family. It may well have been more populous earlier, as the distribution suggests the better land was being concentrated into a few holdings, probably in the hands of tacksmen. At this same time there were 132 people living in the "Crags" between Ardess and Lagline with five families at Nockie and nine at Ruchoss (Rowchoish) when the population was clearly denser in the Highland parts of Buchanan than the Lowland. The period of greatest population in the Highland areas was probably the end of the 17th century and the first half of the 18th century, i.e. before the clearances. In Glen Dubh, as mentioned before, the laird of Bruach Chaoruinn appears to have been the landowner at the lower end, while Comer may have been in separate ownership. The area within the Stronmacnair burying ground is believed to have been reserved for the lairds, while lesser mortals were interred outside.

Later, all the occupants of the glen would be tenants of Montrose, probably through the tacksmen. There was probably still some community organisation and the Tom-a-mhoid (Moot Hill) at Ballimore may well have remained the central meeting point for the glen, even if it was only to decide when the cattle and other livestock would be moved from the low ground to the summer grazings behind the Bein Bhan where the *airidh* summer house ruins can still be found, so that the grass would grow for hay and the few crops be planted. The crops were probably grey oats and bere, a form of barley, with possibly a few potatoes, although the last-named were only grown in the fields in Stirlingshire for the first time in 1728. The main means of livelihood was livestock: cattle, sheep and goats. The cattle were small and black, the sheep, the old white-faced breed, kept in at night and during the winter, and the goats the same as are on Ben Lomond yet. The goats were probably a better source of milk than the cattle, who were only milked in the summer up in the *airidhs*, or sheilings, the milk being made into butter and cheese. The goat-milk cheese is reputed to have been like Parmesan. It was not unkown for rent to be paid in kids, so generally goats were very useful. The cattle were kept mainly for fresh meat and would be bled in the winter.

The houses of poorer people were made of stones and turf and could be put up in three or four days—"poor mean smoky huts without any door or window shutters", let alone glass.

THE DAYS OF THE CLEARANCES: 1745–1800

After the 1745 rebellion, the enlargement of holdings began. There may have been evictions in this area but to begin with it was probably more a matter of not giving new leases of vacant holdings, but letting them to adjacent tenants. In the late 1760's and early 70's, with the boom in wool prices, the black-faced sheep were brought in, and with them the whole character of the country was changed. The sheep required the grazings used by the cattle, so the cattle had to go. The black-faced sheep were hardy and did not require herding or shelter at night or in the winter, so few

11

people were required to look after them, and some of these were English-speaking Lowlanders.

Large numbers of people were displaced from the Highland parts of the parishes of Aberfoyle, Callander and Buchanan. Some found a place working on the moss clearances at Blairdrummond, where, at its peak, 600 were employed, nearly all Gaelic-speaking Highlanders. These were also the great years for the cattle "trysts" at Falkirk. The markets were held annually on the second Tuesday of the months of August, September, and October, and were, of course, in later years, swollen artificially by the selling-off of cattle displaced by the sheep. Normally 10–15,000 cattle were sold, but in some years 30–40,000, together with 15–25,000 sheep, resulting from the increased cattle trade, stimulating the tanning industry and the export of hides from the Forth ports.

At Aberfoyle there were traditionally three fairs, October (*Feill Barachen*) for buying in cattle and hiring servants, April or May for selling cattle and August for the sale of lambs.

At the same time as the changes were taking place in the more remote areas, changes, although possibly more gradual, were being made in the tenure and methods of working the farms with a larger proportion of arable land. Traditionally the lease was held by the tacksman, who usually kept the best land for himself and let the remainder, particularly the land that could not be ploughed and had to be cultivated by hand, to the crofters or cottars. In 1825 there were seven Craiguchty cottaries, each with two acres of arable land and entitled to grazing for two cows and one calf, or equivalent on the hill. Tacksmen in this area existed until 1870.

The arable land was divided into In-field and Out-field, and to provide adequate drainage, was worked on the run-rig system. The raised cultivated rigs were anything from 20–40 feet wide, and the space between was full of stones, and all manner of agricultural weeds, including briars and nettles. The In-field received all the manure from the steadings, and the Out-field usually none. The In-field was continually cropped, most usually with grey oats and barley (usually bere) alternating with occasional crops of flax and peas. A poverty rotation was worked in the Out-field, which extended to the head-dyke. Crops of oats were grown usually for about three years until there was no longer any economic return; there was little enough with the grey oats anyhow as it frequently yielded only three seeds for one planted; then the land was left fallow for 3–6 years.

The enlargement of holdings enabled more efficient methods to be used, although the crofters would cease to be independent, and some must have been displaced altogether. This type of dis-

12

placement was probably most pronounced in the Barony of Drummond. The population of Drymen parish in 1755 was 2,789, in 1792 only 1,607, or a decrease of 55% and this in a predominantly Lowland parish. Buchanan was reduced from 1,699 in 1755 to only 636 by 1811, or 62.5%. In Aberfoyle parish, a much less populated area, the decrease was only 11%, from 895 to 790, although by 1841 the figure was down to 549.

The areas least affected immediately by these changes were probably the parts of Gartloaning, Duchray and Achray, where there had never been much land suitable for cultivation and the grazing was not very suitable for sheep. The traditional farming of this area was dealing in, and particularly wintering, cattle in the shelter of the "ravines and woods". Some cattle were brought in for fattening on the summer grazings in May, and a certain amount of bog-hay would be made; but the main stocks were brought in, in October and sold again in the spring at a profit of £1–£2 per head.

By 1799, the Rev. J. Robertson, D.D., minister of Callander, was able to say—"many farmers now live in houses"—"very few want for glass windows." These new houses were built when leases were renewed. "When a farmer gets a new house, of two floors, he commonly reserves the low house, in which he formerly lived, for his servants." But there were still a few of the old type of establishment—"where the farmer and cattle lodge under the same roof, with separate entries and only a partition between them".

THE PERIOD 1800–1930

At the beginning of the 19th century, although Gaelic was still chiefly spoken and—"Ancient Highland dress is very generally worn"—most people understood English. The Rev. P. Grahame, D.D., of Aberfoyle, was able to report that although they were still—"little employed in cultivating the ground"—"the character of the Highlander is rapidly assimilating itself to that of his neighbours in the south and east". Even so, there was still a small garrison at Inversnaid at the time of the Statistical Account in 1792, and the site was retained by the military authorities until the 1820's.

The gradual enlargement of holdings continued throughout the 19th century and agriculture developed on much the same pattern until the present. It is of interest that the land rental values were much higher in the 19th century than 100 years later, especially when one allows for the changing value of money.

Holding	1825	1927
Frenich	£270—Thomas Grahame	£70—Hugh Campbell, retired 1959
Blairhullichan	£125—Duncan Grahame	£72—James Kerr
Achray and Grahavie	£475—Mal. MacFarlane	£125—Peter Buchanan

The decreasing population trend was halted by the commercial development of the slate quarries, north of Aberfoyle. In 1820 only three men employed, in 1834 twenty men. In 1847 Peter McKeich was the tenant—McKeich's still live in the old school house, and one son works in Achray Forest. But the quarry was made into a company in 1858 and was soon the third largest quarry in Scotland, producing 1,400,000 slates annually. Production stopped finally in 1951. The slate industry attracted the railway, which was opened in 1885. Further employment also resulted from the Glasgow Corporation impounding Loch Katrine as a reservoir. The first aqueduct, completed in 1859, is on a gradient of 10 inches per mile, and can supply 40 million gallons per day. The more direct aqueduct, opened in 1885, is at $11\frac{1}{2}$ inches per mile, and can supply 70 million gallons per day. The compensation water developments affected much good grazing land at the head of Loch Venachar, which was raised $5\frac{3}{4}$ inches; Loch Drunkie was raised 25 feet.

The change from crofting to sheep was not the only development that took place in the second half of the 18th century. Until that time the woodlands had been of little value except for the manufacture of a certain amount of birch charcoal for iron smelting. At first the iron was brought to the charcoal, but latterly the charcoal was probably transported to the lowlands. Transport overland was by pack ponies, so areas where water transport was possible were preferred. This industry declined with the introduction of coke smelting about 1760. By neglect and destructive grazing by cattle and goats, the natural birch and oak mixed woodlands must have virtually disappeared by mid-17th century, except in the areas of limited population and on steep rocky faces, and these would only be sparse scrub for the most part.

There was, however, an increasing demand for oak-bark for the developing tanning industry, stimulated by the increased cattle trade and export of hides from the Forth ports. The Duke of Montrose quickly appreciated the value of oak coppice woodlands. The market began to develop between 1760 and 1770 and by the beginning of the next century there were 3,000 acres of oak coppice in Stirlingshire; 1,800 acres in the Buchanan woods alone, and 100 on Duchray Estate owned by General Grahame, Stirling.

In 1809 the price was £18 per ton and a yield of about $1\frac{1}{2}$–2 tons per acre was usual. The bark only was valuable since at this time oak was rarely used for charcoal. Although some wood was used for making wheel spokes and rafters, and withies in basket making, much more was wasted. Because of this, wood distillation to secure chemicals such as acetates as well as charcoal, now again in demand, was later developed. At first these plants were semi-

14

portable and moved with the annual cutting blocks or "hags". Latterly, when the tan bark market began to fail, due to cheap imports of foreign bark extracts, the Duke of Montrose operated a plant at Balmaha. This plant closed just before the First World War. Most of the oak woods were established by planting. On bare ground, nurse trees were used, including broom and conifers. Sometimes the nurses were planted a few years before, and the oak introduced at a fourteen-foot square spacing; most of the nurses were removed when about fifteen years old. Generally, on Montrose Estates, the trees were planted in mixture, with the following quantities per acre, 1,000 hardwood (sycamore, beech and ash in some areas in addition to oak), 1,200 Scots pines and 900 European larches. The men semi-pitted the hardwood and planted about 300 per day. The conifers were L-notched and 600–700 were planted per day. The pay was 12½p per day and it took about five days to plant one acre. By this method, the Montrose Estate planted 1,200 acres in 20 years.

Under the Dukes of Montrose the area developed considerably—industry was encouraged, new roads built and others improved, notably the Aberfoyle–Ward Toll–Ballat Road in 1810–20, and the Aberfoyle–Achray (Duke's Road) in 1820.

In 1925 the estates were formed into a company, Montrose Estates Ltd., and in 1926 the Dowager Duchess sold "all and whole" of the Earldom of Menteith to the Company. In 1929 the lands in the parishes of Aberfoyle and Port were offered for sale. The Forestry Commission bought Renagour and Gartloaning. Blairhullichan and Frenich were bought by the heirs of Allan R. Smith. In 1929 Sir A. Kay Muir bought Dounans and Achray, but sold to the Forestry Commission in 1931, when the Duke's Road was opened to the public. The remaining areas, Blairhullichan, Frenich, Rowardennan, and Duchray and part of the Trossachs, have all been acquired since 1945.

POPULATION FIGURES

Parish	1755	1800	Year 1811	1841	1930
Aberfoyle	895	790	—	549	1,134
Buchanan	1,699	748	636	—	—
Drymen	2,789	1,608	1,652	—	—

15

BIBLIOGRAPHY

AITON, W.	*Labouring and Crofting of Moss Earth*—(1800–1814)
ANON.	*The Trials of James Duncan and Robert MacGregor, Three Sons of the Celebrated Rob Roy before the High Court of Justiciary, in the years 1752, 1753 and 1754*— H. Hay & Co., Edinburgh—1818
BUCHANAN, W. (ACHMAR)	*The History of the Ancient Surname of Buchanan*—1793
Catholic Encyclopaedia	
COWAN, S.	*Three Celtic Earldoms*
DUN, P.	*Summer at the Lake of Menteith*—1866
DRUMMOND	*Genealogy of the House of Drummond*—1831
FRASER, SIR WM.	*The Red Book of Menteith*—1880
GRAEME, L. G.	*Or and Sable*—1903
GRAHAM, ALEX., OF DUCHRAY	*Description of Six Parishes in Perthshire*—1724— MacFarlane Papers—Scottish National Library
GRAHAM, REV. P.	*Agriculture in Stirlingshire*—1816
GRAHAM, REV. P.	*Sketches of Perthshire*—1806
GRAHAM, NICOL	*An Inquiry into the Causes which facilitate the Rise and Progress of Rebellions in the Highlands of Scotland*— 1747—Gartmore MS. Extract in *Don Roberto, Biography of Robert Bontine Cunningham-Graham*
GUTHRIE SMITH	*History of Strathendrick*
HAMILTON	*Highland Constable*—1953
HUTCHESON	*Lake of Menteith*—Mackay—1899
JOYNSON, MAJOR W.	Personal Papers
KIRK, ROBERT	*The Secret Commonwealth*
MACGREGOR, STIRLING	*Notes, Historical and Descriptive, on the Priory of Inchmahome*—1815
MACGREGOR, AMELIA G. M.	*The History of the Clan Gregor*
MACNAIR, P.	*Perthshire*—1912
MACFARLANE, JAMES	*History of Clan MacFarlane*—1922
MacFarlane Geographical Series	*Parishes of Aberfoyle, Callander, Buchanan, etc.*— Scottish National Library
MALCOLM, D.	*Memoirs of the House of Drummond*—1808
MARSHALL	*Historic Scenes in Perthshire*—Oliphant—1880
O'HANLON, REV. J. C.	*Lives of the Irish Saints*—Vol. II
PINKERTON	*History of Scotland Preceding 1056*
ROBERTSON, REV. J.	*General View of Agriculture in the County of Perth*—1799
Statistical Account (old)	1793—Parishes of Aberfoyle, Drymen, Buchanan and Callander
Statistical Account (new)	1845—Parishes of Aberfoyle, Drymen, Buchanan and Callander

MAPS OF THE AREA

1630	*Gordon Manuscript* (Timothy Pont Survey)—Menteith—Scottish National Library
1654	*Geographie Blavianae*—*Blaeu's Atlas of Europe*—Lennox (or Shire of Dunbritton)
1745–55	Roy Manuscript—British Museum (Photoprint—Scottish National Library)
1777	Ross, Charles of Greenlaw—*Map of Dunbarton*
1783	Stobie, J.—*Map of Perthshire*

16

1817	Grassom, J.—*County of Stirling*
1866	Ordnance Survey: 6 inches to mile series
1949	Ordnance Survey. Tourist Map: *The Trossachs and Loch Lomond*: 1 inch to 1 mile (HMSO, price 50p)
1951	Ordnance Survey. Sheet 53, *Loch Lomond*, Sheet 54, *Stirling*: 1 inch to 1 mile (HMSO, price 40p per sheet)

APPENDIX

SELECTED LIST OF PLACES IN CHARTER TO MALISE GRAHAME
IN 1427

Charter Name	Present Name	Remarks
Craynis Estir ⎱ Craynis Wester ⎰	Part of Aberfoyle Village	"Over Creance" in Montrose records Behind Episcopal Church?
Craguthy Estir	——	West end of village. Seven cottaries
Craguthy Wester	Craiguchty	*Circa* 1825
Glasswerde	Glassart	Old Glassart east of Drumlean
Drumlaen	Drumlean	Old spelling conforms to modern pronunciation
Ledarde	Ledard	
Gartnerthynach	Gartnerichnich	
Blaerereruscanys	Blairuskins	No doubt included "Teapot"
Foreste of Baith Sidis of Lochcon	——	
Blaeretuchane	Blairhullichan	
Culyingarth	Couligarten	
Frisesleware	?	Fri-(s)-es-le-(w)-are. Discheratyre occurs later. Small water-side grazings?
Rose	Blar an Ross	
Cragmuk	Craigmuick	Craigie usually
Inchere	Inchrie	Ruins opposite school
Gartinhagel	Kirkton	"Gart-an-eaglais"
Bobfresle	Bofrieshlie	Bo-fri-es(h)-lie. Hut-small-water flood?
Bovento	Boninty	"v" may be a mistake
Downans	Dounans	
Baleth	Balleich	
Tereochane	——	Terras Lochtoun—Achray?
Drombay	Drumbuidhe	South end Loch Drunkie
Crancafy	Crahavie	S.W. end Loch Venachar
Achray	Achray	Loch Achray Hotel
Glassel ⎱ Cravaneculy ⎰	Glaschoile ⎱ Crantullich ⎰	South side Loch Katrine
Brigend	——	Bridgend, Gartmore?
Lonanys	Gartloaning	
Drumanust	——	Drum an east, or west?
Schanghil	Shannochill	
Ernelty	Arnachily	
Monabrachys	Monievreckies	brack = breac = spotted = speckled moorland
Gartmulne	——	Mill of Malling
Erncomy	Arntomy	
Achmore	——	Great field?
Port Inche	Portend Island	Inch Talla or later Talla

17

High on the south, huge Benvenue
Down on the lake in masses threw
Crags, knolls and mounds, confusedly hurl'd
The fragments of an earlier world.

—Scott, *The Lady of the Lake.*

GEOLOGY

By Dr. Basil C. King

THE greater part of the Forest Park lies within typical Highlands, but a small portion along the south-eastern border belongs to the Midland Valley of Scotland. These divisions are as significant geologically as they are obvious topographically. The boundary between them is marked by a major structural dislocation named the Highland Boundary Fault.

An understanding of the geology of the area is best achieved by a consideration of its geological history, which falls broadly into two chapters, although these are very unequal in length. The first was a long period of geological time, from some 500 to 200 million years ago, during which the various rock formations, which constitute the "solid" geology, were successively laid down and subjected to a number of earth movements resulting in their present more or less complicated structures. The second was very much more recent and only relates to the last few tens of millions of years of earth history. It is the record of the sculpturing of the present landscape of mountains, hills, valleys and lochs by the action of

18

running water and moving ice from a land mass constructed of the various rock formations formed during the earlier period. The great interval of time between these two chapters has left virtually no record in the history of this area, but is very well documented farther south, where it is represented by a great range of strata from the familiar Coal Measures of the Midland Valley of Scotland, and elsewhere in Britain, to the Chalk of southern England.

THE HIGHLAND ROCKS

Much of the area is underlain by a group of rocks referred to as the Dalradian Series, which in fact constitute the greater part of the Central Highlands, and were therefore appropriately named after the ancient Scottish Kingdom of Dalriada. This series was originally a succession of sediments laid down in shallow seas, consisting of gravels, sands, muds, and so forth, which in due course became compacted to form grits, sandstones and shales. Subsequently, as a result of strong compression during earth movements, these rocks acquired a cleavage or foliation, while in response to elevated temperature the original constituents have in varying degree recrystallised into larger grains or combined to form new minerals. Rocks having these characters are termed metamorphic. The cleavage or foliation is marked by the appearance of a series of strong partings or even a banding of the minerals, together with an ability to split readily into parallel sheets. It is much more prominent in the finer grained rocks developed from original shales than in those from coarser sandstones and grits.

In this area, moreover, there is very well seen the effects of progressive metamorphism in the Dalradians, metamorphism by pressure being everywhere in evidence, but recrystallisation due to heat showing a fairly rapid increase as the rocks are traced northwestwards from the Highland Border. Thus in a belt extending from just north of Aberfoyle to the vicinity of Luss the original shales are in the condition of slates with a well-marked cleavage, but with the mineral constituents retaining their former fine-grained character. At both of these localities the rocks have been worked as roofing slates. Along the north-western margin of the slate belt the rocks show a bright sheen on the cleavage surfaces due to the development of thin flakes of white mica and are referred to as phyllites. Still further to the north-west, as around Rowardennan, Ben Lomond and Loch Katrine, rocks which had the same initial character have been further recrystallised into schists, in which the new mineral grains are sufficiently large to be readily distinguished. Mica is very prominent and the flakes of this mineral have a parallel arrangement giving the rock a characteristic schistosity, or, if also

19

banded, a foliation. The dark mica, biotite, becomes increasingly conspicuous in the coarser schists. Often, as may be seen to the north of Loch Chon, the layers show crumpling due to later movements, while lenticles and veins of quartz are common.

Coarser grained rocks derived from former grits and sandstones are also abundant in the area. Near the Highland Border from Aberfoyle to just north of Balmaha the rocks show little metamorphism, and the original grit or sand grains are clearly visible; but farther north, as on Ben Venue and Ben Ledi and on parts of Ben Lomond, the prevailing rocks are termed schistose grits, for the finer matrix between the grit fragments, has been recrystallised to form mica and related minerals. The grit fragments are predominantly of quartz, but felspar and slaty or schistose material are also found.

In a number of localities, as, for example, to the south-east of Ben Lomond, on either side of Loch Chon, and around the south-eastern end of Loch Katrine, belts of darker coloured rocks, termed "Green Beds", occur. These contain a high proportion of lime- and magnesia-rich minerals, such as chlorite, epidote and, sometimes, hornblende. Their origin is not certain, but it has been suggested that they are sediments derived from basic igneous rocks.

The general arrangement of the Dalradian Series in the area is comparatively simple. Thus the main groups of rocks as shown on the map are disposed in belts trending approximately N.E.-S.W., so that different groups of rocks are successively encountered in traversing the area at right angles to this direction of "strike". From the Highland Border at Aberfoyle one passes in turn over the groups known respectively as Leny Grits, Aberfoyle Slates, and Ben Ledi Grits and Schists. It is to be emphasised, however that in detail the succession is much more complicated and the representatives of most rock types enter in varying degree into these larger groups, which have been defined primarily for convenience in mapping and classification. This may in part be judged from the map and section (Figs. 1 and 2), but is even more readily apparent from the examination of any section in the area where reasonably continuous exposures are seen, as along the shore of Loch Lomond near Rowardennan, along the Trossachs road from Aberfoyle, and in the cuttings along the aqueduct road towards Loch Katrine.

The inclination of the beds shows in the main a progressive variation from almost vertical near the Highland Border to more gentle south-easterly dips in the north-west of the area. This was originally interpreted as implying that successively underlying or older formations are encountered towards the north-west. An understanding of the sequence of formations in the Dalradian Series is complicated by the absence of fossils, and the consequent difficulty

20

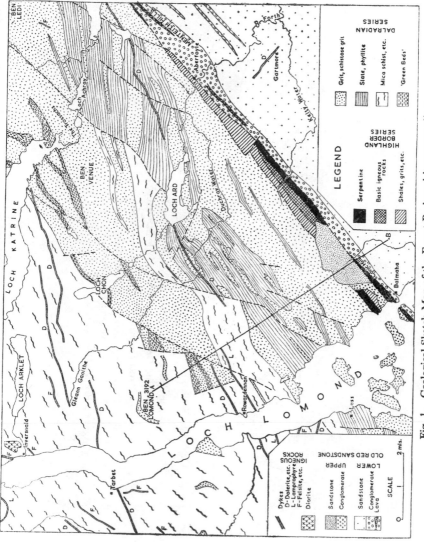

Fig. 1. Geological Sketch Map of the Forest Park and its surroundings.

LEGEND

DALRADIAN SERIES

▨ Grit, schistose grit
▥ Slate, phyllite
▧ Mica schist, etc.
▦ 'Green Beds'

HIGHLAND BORDER SERIES

■ Serpentine
▨ Basic igneous rocks
▨ Shales, grits, etc.

OLD RED SANDSTONE

IGNEOUS ROCKS

Dykes
D – Dolerite, etc.
L – Lamprophyre
F – Felsite, etc.

Diorite

UPPER
Sandstone
Conglomerate

LOWER
Sandstone
Conglomerate
Lava

SCALE

0 ___ 1 ___ 2 mls.

21

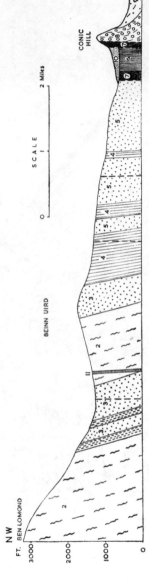

Fig. 2. Geological Section from Ben Lomond to Conic Hill along the line A—B in Fig. 1.

Dalradian Series: 1—'Green Beds', 2 and 3—Ben Ledi
Schists and Grits: 4 and 5—Aberfoyle Slates and Leny Grits

Highland Border Series: 6—Shale, grit, 7—Serpentine

Old Red Sandstone: Lower: 8—Conglomerate, 9—Sandstone
Upper: 10—Sandstone

Igneous Rocks: 11—Dykes

of correlating rocks between one district and another. Moreover, it is known that the arrangement of the beds results from intense folding before Old Red Sandstone times, but the style of the folding on a large scale is a matter of conjecture, and many different views have been expressed on this problem. Nevertheless, in some parts of the Highlands huge overfolds involving large-scale inversions of strata can be demonstrated, while in others it can sometimes be shown that apparently simple structures must in fact be more complex. Thus, from the evidence provided by sedimentation features, such as graded and current bedding, it has recently been shown that the Aberfoyle Slates are actually older than both the grit groups which flank them. A large close fold must therefore be postulated, with a repetition of beds of corresponding ages on each side of the axis, the Leny and Ben Ledi grits being equivalent formations.

HIGHLAND BORDER SERIES

Forming a narrow wedge against the Highland Boundary Fault occurs a series of unmetamorphosed grits and shales, shown by the evidence of fossils to be of Cambrian and Ordovician age. Their precise relationship with the Dalradians is somewhat doubtful, since mutual junctions are always faulted, but they are evidently to be regarded as the latest of the sedimentary formations entering into the make-up of the Highlands. Together with the sediments there occur basic lavas and basic and ultrabasic intrusive rocks, of which serpentine is the most characteristic, while bands of jasper are found in places. These rocks may be seen between Aberfoyle and the headstreams of the Kelty Water, but are more readily accessible outside the Park, near the shore a short distance to the north of Balmaha.

OLD RED SANDSTONE

Rocks of this system are largely confined to the south-east of the Highland Boundary Fault and were laid down as scree, torrent and possibly lake deposits in continental basins on the flanks of the newly formed mountains which were being carved out of the folded Dalradian rocks. The Lower Old Red Sandstone commences with conglomerates containing closely packed pebbles and rounded boulders, often of very large size, and is continued by great thicknesses of brown and purplish sandstones which underlie the fertile pastures and arable land between the Campsie Fells and the Highland Border. There then occured a further period of earth movements during which the rocks of the Lower Old Red Sandstone were gently folded, while extensive faulting took place. Chief among the faults is the Highland Boundary Fault itself, which extends in a very nearly straight line from Stonehaven to Helensburgh, passing through the Park in the neighbourhood of Aberfoyle and thence towards Balmaha. Along this line the Lower Old Red Sandstone has been let down against the Dalradians or the Highland Border Series, the entire Midland Valley of Scotland being a downfaulted belt in which formations younger than those of the Highlands have been preserved. The Highland Boundary Fault is generally of the compressional or "reversed" type, along which the adjacent Old Red Sandstone has been sharply upturned, so that the lowest members of the system, the conglomerates, are here exposed. These, being resistant to erosion, form a prominent line of hills at the present day, notably the Menteith Hills, near Aberfoyle, and Conic Hill, near Balmaha.

Other faults formed at about this time produced sharp dislocations in the Dalradian rocks, often occupied by crush zones, which have had an important influence in the development of the present day valleys. Moreover, it is often apparent from the displacements shown by steeply dipping formations that movement has been horizontal as well as vertical.

A period of uplift and erosion followed the post-Lower Old Red Sandstone movements, which was in turn succeeded by the deposition of the Upper Old Red Sandstone within the more extensive basins of a maturely denuded landscape. The Upper Old Red Sandstone, consisting of pebble beds and sandstones, generally of a bright red colour, remains largely in its original horizontal condition and rests on the eroded edges of the folded Dalradian or Lower Old Red strata. It has been preserved from more recent erosion only in comparatively few localities, notably in the flat-lying moorlands to the north of Conic Hill. The structural relations here show that further movement occured along the Highland Boundary Fault, but this time with a smaller northward downthrow, so that Upper Old Red Sandstone is only preserved on the north side of the fault. (See geological section, Fig. 2).

IGNEOUS ROCKS

During Lower Old Red Sandstone times lavas and volcanic ashes were extruded to form the great thicknesses building the Ochils, and represented as an insignificant scale in the Menteith Hills. At about the same time the Dalradians were in many districts invaded by great masses of granite, together with subordinate diorite and other coarsely crystalline igneous rocks, as well as by numerous smaller dykes and sheets of related but finer grained rocks. A few such dykes of felsite and lamprophyre are to be found within the area, while a small mass of diorite occurs at Inversnaid, not far beyond the limits of the Park.

Plate 12.   Ben Lomond summit in snow; the southward view towards Luss and its islets.

Plate 13.   The northward view from Ben Lomond's snow-clad summit, towards Ben Lui and the neighbouring peaks.

Plate 14. Ben Lomond seen across the loch from Inveruglas.

Plate 15. The Loch Lomond steamer *Maid of the Loch* sails through the narrows near Rowardennan.

Plate 16. The beach at Mullarochy Bay, amid the oakwoods, between Balmaha and Rowardennan.

Plate 17. Paddlers on the beach beside the Rowardennan Camp Site.

Plate 18. Forest workers' timber houses near Sallochy in the Rowardennan woods on Loch Lomondside.

Plate 19. Ruins of croft houses at Wester Sallochy, a settlement abandoned about 1820.

Plate 20.   Craigmore Hill at Aberfoyle.

Plate 21.   The wooded shores of Loch Katrine, seen from the summit of Ben Venue.

Plate 22.   Loch Dubh and its farmstead, backed by the young woods of Loch Ard Forest, between Aberfoyle and Stronachlachar.

Plate 23.   A noontide picnic beside the Duke's Road, between Aberfoyle and the Trossachs.

Plate 24.   Loch Ard, with distant Ben Lomond rising beyond.

Plate 25.   Pine-clad crags above Loch Katrine, near the Trossachs steamer pier.

At a later date, towards the end of Carboniferous or in early Permian times, numbers of broad persistent dykes of dark, medium-grained dolerite, having nearly E.-W. trends, were injected into the rocks of the Scottish Midland Valley and the adjacent parts of the Highlands. Several of these dykes may be seen in the Park, notably two to the south of Loch Katrine and one extending to the east and west of Loch Ard.

EVOLUTION OF THE PRESENT LANDSCAPE

Study of the pattern of the present river systems shows that the topography of the region as we know it to-day may be considered to have originated when, perhaps in mid- or late-Tertiary times, a planed-down surface cutting alike across hard and soft formations was elevated to form a plateau with a gentle south-easterly tilt. With this slope developed the earliest or "consequent" streams, now represented by parts of Loch Lomond, Loch Chon to Loch Ard, and the extremities of Loch Katrine.

As erosion proceeded, however, the great variations in the hardness of the underlying rocks exercised an increasing influence, determining the courses of the secondary or "subsequent" streams. These were excavated along softer formations, such as the schists and slates, rather than the schistose grits or quartzites in the Dalradians, and along the softer sandstones of the Old Red Sandstone. In very many cases, too, rivers followed the shatter belts along faults in the Highland rocks, a number of examples being easily recognised on the map.

Conversely, the more resistant formations were left as erosion relics and now constitute the more prominent mountains, the summits of the highest of which most nearly approximate to the surface of the original plateau. Such mountains are Ben Lomond, Ben Venue, and Ben Ledi, partly or wholly formed of tougher schistose grits, and the Menteith Hills, composed of Lower Old Red conglomerates.

Elevation of the region was actually intermittent, a notable pause occuring when the sea, and consequently the base level to which the rivers were downcutting, stood 1,000 to 1,200 feet above its present level. This stage is reflected in the mature profiles of the upper reaches of many of the rivers, such as Gleann Gaothie, to the north of Ben Lomond. A lower and correspondingly later temporary base level is represented by the valley occupied by Loch Chon and Loch Ard, and also that filled by Loch Katrine. In each case further elevation led to the renewal of downcutting from the seaward ends of the rivers, so that in most cases the valleys possess composite profiles, rapids or falls marking the present positions reached by headward erosion of the successively rejuvenated portions of the rivers. Although the general configuration of the hills and valleys has resulted from sculpturing by running water, the rugged grandeur of the mountains, the broad clear straths and valleys, and the very existence of the lochs are the direct consequence of powerful remoulding by ice. During the Pleistocene Ice Age mountain sides were excavated and the rocks denuded of soil and rock waste, the existing valleys were widened and scoured, often "over-deepened", while mounds and barrages of rocky debris were left behind in their lower reaches on the disappearance of the ice. With the return of a milder climate the broad U-shaped valleys were reoccupied by rivers and streams, while numerous lochs formed in the over-deepened portions or were impounded by barriers of glacial debris.

The widening of the pre-glacial valleys also led to the truncation of spurs and the removal of the lower courses of tributary streams, which now appear as "hanging" valleys, descending abruptly into the main valley by way of waterfalls. This is well displayed by all the streams flowing westwards into Loch Lomond, the most spectacular example being at Inversnaid.

Among the last aspects of geological history have been further erosions by the rivers, together with the re-sorting of glacial drift and the deposition of alluvium on the floors of the valleys. Most rapid deposition is occuring where the rivers carrying their load of sediments are checked on entering the numerous lochs. These in consequence are silting up at their headward ends and becoming constricted where small deltas are formed at the entry of tributary streams.

Finally as a geological agent must be reckoned Man, who has emulated Nature's work in damming the valleys to form or enlarge lochs. It is interesting to note, however, that use has necessarily been made of the upper mature courses of river profiles, as in the case of Loch Katrine, or of "hanging" valleys, as at Loch Arklet, to secure the required "head" of water in the location of reservoirs.

The geology of the area is shown on the following maps published by the Geological Survey of Great Britain:
Sheet 38 (Loch Lomond) 1-inch to the mile (hand-coloured edition; not at present available).
Sheet 14 (Firth of Clyde) 4 miles to the inch.
Publications dealing with the area include especially:

GREGORY, J. W.	1928: The Geology of Loch Lomond. *Transactions of the Geological Society of Glasgow*. Vol. 18, p. 301
GREGORY, J. W.	1931: *Dalradian Geology*, London
McCALLIEN, W. J.	1938: *Geology of Glasgow and District*, Glasgow.
READ, H. H. and MacGREGOR, A. G.	1948: *British Regional Geology: The Grampian Highlands* (2nd Edition). Geological Survey of Great Britain

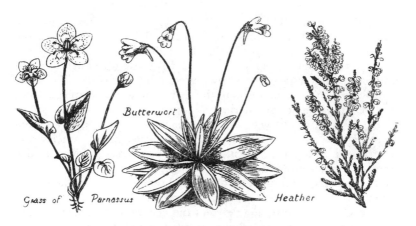

Butterwort

Grass of Parnassus

Heather

Land of brown heath and shaggy wood,
Land of the mountain and the flood.

—Scott, *The Lay of the Last Minstrel.*

THE BOTANY OF THE AREA

By Dr. D. Patton

In the lines quoted above, Sir Walter Scott gives a very concise summary of the topography, climatic conditions and ecology of the area as a whole. The configuration of the district is characteristic of a much-dissected tableland. This, at the higher altitudes, shows a wealth of corries and escarpments, the rock-ledges of which are the home of arctic-alpine plants; whilst the screes, boulder clay and alluvium in the valleys provide soils of great variety, depending mainly upon their origin and water content. The climatic conditions, too, are as varied as they are uncertain. In some parts the average annual rainfall is over 100 inches; but in spite of its abundance it becomes less available to the vegetation of the upper areas on account of the low temperatures often obtaining there. Cloud and mist impede sunlight and have their effect upon plant life. Snow lies long upon the mountains. All things considered there is a great diversity both of species and of plant associations and ample scope for the study of ecology.

THE MOUNTAIN FLORA

The two highest mountains of the area are Ben Lomond (3,192 feet) with the Ptarmigan (2,398 feet), and Ben Venue with its twin peaks (2,393 and 2,386 feet respectively). Ben Lomond, being the higher as well as the more frequented, will serve to illustrate the mountain flora. From Aberfoyle, this eminence appears decidedly conical, but from the south and west it looms up as a long and gradually rising massif topped by a great crowning cone. This cone is truncated on the north, where there are extensive precipices. Seen from Loch Lomond in the autumn, the ben stands out in all its glory, the colour of its vegetation giving a clue to its geology as well as to its botany. The zonation is well marked and characteristic. The lowest zone of bracken, *Pteridium aquilinum*, golden in dry weather, russet-brown during a wet spell, extends from the wooded shore upwards to an altitude of about 1,600 feet, where the colour indicates a different association. There the purple of the heather or ling, *Calluna vulgaris*, zone girdles the ben, and in its turn merges into the green of the blaeberry, *Vaccinium myrtillus* zone. Above this lies the arctic-alpine grassland which continues towards the mountain-top detritus.

Although arctic-alpine botanists prefer to go further north in Scotland, to where the Laoigh-Lawers-Caenlochan Schists outcrop, Ben Lomond offers a very good boreal flora, well above the average of those other mountains which consist of quartz-mica schists and quartzites.

Many Glasgow botanists would rather climb Ben Lomond by the Bealach Buidhe Burn which enters the loch to the north of Rowardennan Pier, than by the path which starts near the hotel. The source of this stream is not far from the summit, and its descent is more or less direct, thus affording an excellent section of the vegetation regions. Again, because of the abundance of water, the escarpments abutting on the stream bear a luxurious growth and plant life is seen at its best. As the burn is approached from the pier, a good patch of the slender rush, *Juncus tenuis*, may be observed. It is when the burn is reached, however, that the real botanising begins. The yellow saxifrage, *Saxifraga aizoides*, has come down to the lochside, and before the one thousand foot contour is passed the alpine lady's mantle, *Alchemilla alpina*, has appeared. In this section the following will be amongst the plants noted:—

Globe flower, *Trollius europaeus;* purging flax, *Linum cartharticum;* stone bramble, *Rubus saxatilis;* tormentil, *Potentilla erecta;* starry saxifrage, *Saxifraga stellaris;* mossy saxifrage, *S. hypnoides;* angelica, *Angelica sylvestris;* smooth heath bedstraw, *Galium saxatile;* cross-leaved bedstraw, *G. boreale;* golden rod, *Solidago virgaurea;* louseworts, *Pedicularis palustris* and *P. sylvatica;* ribwort plantain, *Plantago lanceolata;* the filmy ferns, *Hymenophyllum tunbridgense* and *H. unilaterale;* and the least club-moss, *Selaginella selaginoides.*

By the time the *Calluna-Vaccinium* region has been reached, *Alchemilla alpina* has become more abundant and other arctic-alpines have appeared, e.g., the viviparous persicaria or alpine bistort, *Polygonum viviparum*, which "anticipates" a failure to set seeds, by producing bulbils as well as florets on its inflorescence; the alpine meadow rue, *Thalictrum alpinum;* and the alpine sorrel, *Oxyria digyna.*

Botanically the most interesting region lies between the two-thousand foot contour and the summit. It may be divided into two according to its configuration:—

1. The open mountain slopes, up to the mountain-top detritus; the upper grasslands.
2. The crags and corries with their pockets, ledges and fissures.

THE UPPER GRASSLANDS

On Ben Lomond these are mostly confined to the southern slopes. Unlike the lower reaches, they have a well-drained soil which is kept moist for most of the year by the large number of springs that occur at different altitudes. They lack the stagnation of the lower slopes. Besides, the soil is more or less stable and produces a great variety of plants varying in species according to the habitat, e.g.:—

Thalictrum alpinum; lesser marsh marigold, *Caltha minor;* alpine mouse-ear chickweed, *Cerastium alpinum;* mossy cyphel, *Cherleria sedoides; Alchemilla alpina;* procumbent sibbaldia, *Sibbaldia procumbens;* cloudberry, *Rubus chamaemorus; Linum catharticum;* dwarf cudweed, *Gnaphalium supinum;* blaeberry, *Vaccinium myrtillus;* cowberry, *V. vitis-idaea;* greater blaeberry, *V. uliginosum;* crowberry, *Empetrum nigrum;* least willow, *Salix herbacea;* lesser twayblade, *Listera cordata;* Scottish asphodel, *Tofieldia palustris;* viviparous sheep's fescue, *Festuca ovina* var. *vivipara;* alpine hair-grass, *Deschampsia alpina;* blue moor-grass, *Sesleria caerulea;* alpine meadow-grass, *Poa alpina;* mat-grass, *Nardus stricta;* parsley fern, *Cryptogramme crispa;* fir club-moss, *Lycopodium selago;* alpine club-moss, *L. alpinum*, and staghorn moss, *L. clavatum.*

THE CRAGS AND CORRIES

The vegetation of the ledges and fissures of the upper escarpments is, in season, the glory of the ben. Here is Nature's rock garden with festoons of the purple saxifrage and pockets abloom with flowers. Although many of the plants mentioned for the upper grassland are found here, the vegetation of the crags has to withstand a greater range of temperatures; for, while the grasslands may be under snow, which protects them, the escarpments are more often clear of snow, so that by night the crag plants are subjected to considerably lower temperatures.

29

The plants which contribute most to the beauty of the escarpments on Ben Lomond are the purple saxifrage, *Saxifraga oppositifolia;* the globe flower, *Trollius europaeus;* wood cranesbill, *Geranium sylvaticum;* mossy campion, *Silene acaulis;* red campion, *Lychnis dioica;* mountain pansy, *Viola lutea;* wild thyme, *Thymus serpyllum,* and the holly fern, *Polystichum lonchitis.* Also present are:—The twisted-podded whitlow grass, *Draba incana,* and its variety *confusa;* Alpine scurvy-grass, *Cochlearia alpina; Cerastium alpinum; Cherleria sedoides; Sibbaldia procumbens; Saxifraga nivalis; S. stellaris; S. hypnoides;* alpine willowherb, *Epilobium alpinum;* reticulate willow, *Salix reticulata;* the frog orchis, *Habenaria viridis;* Scottish asphodel, *Tofieldia palustris;* the rushes, *Juncus trifidus* and *J. triglumis;* mountain woodrush, *Luzula spicata;* the sedges, *Carex atrata* and *C. rigida;* green spleenwort, *Asplenium viride;* mountain bladder fern, *Cystopteris montana;* moonwort, *Botrychium lunaria,* and interrupted clubmoss, *Lycopodium annotinum.* Even plants of the Lowlands are found here, such as wood anemone, *Anemone nemorosa;* wood sorrel, *Oxalis acetosella;* common lady's mantle, *Alchemilla vulgaris;* harebell, *Campanula rotundifolia,* and the common sorrel, *Rumex acetosa.* Seaside plants such as thrift or sea-pink, *Armeria maritima;* sea plantain, *Plantago maritima,* and rose-root, *Sedum rosea,* which are accustomed to endure a physiological drought, also flourish here.

The flora of the mountain top is dominated by mosses and lichens, chief among the former being *Rhacomitrium lanuginosum.* Growing in the nooks and crannies are the rush, *Juncus trifidis,* the woodrush, *Luzula spicata,* and the sedge, *Carex rigida.* But where the soil is more stable, the bedstraw, *Galium saxatile;* the grass, *Festuca ovina;* the willow, *Salix herbacea;* patches of the cudweed, *Gnaphalium supinum;* and cushions of the campion, *Silene acaulis,* find a roothold.

THE LOCHSIDE FLORA OF LOCH LOMOND

Between Inversnaid and Rowardennan the mountains rise so steeply from the loch that there is no strand except in a few coves; in fact, for a great part of the way, the mountain sides go sheer down into the loch (fjord-like). Botanising here is rather strenuous, as there is no well-defined track, and the scrub amongst the trees is in places very dense. The slopes are well clothed with natural woodland, oak and birch being locally dominant, with hazel and alder frequent and an occasional ash, beech and yew. Outstanding plants are:—Globe flower; climbing corydalis, *Corydalis claviculata;* tutsan, *Hypericum androsaemum;* small upright St. John's-wort, *H. pulchrum;* wood crane's-bill, *Geranium sylvaticum;* stone bramble, *Rubus saxatilis;* and yellow cow-wheat, *Melampyrum pratense.* From

Rowardennan towards Balmaha the shore broadens out and the woodlands provide a more varied vegetation. By the streamlets entering the loch, the alien monkey-flower, *Mimulus luteus;* hemlock water-dropwort, *Oenanthe crocata;* meadow-sweet, *Spiraea ulmaria;* butterwort, *Pinguicula vulgaris;* round-leaved sundew, *Drosera rotundifolia;* bugle, *Ajuga reptans;* and the yellow flag, *Iris pseudacorus,* may be seen. The sand by the loch produces the shore-weed, *Littorella uniflora;* lesser spearwort, *Ranunculus flammula;* pill-wort, *Pilularia globulifera;* and, under water, quill-wort, *Isoetes lacustris.* Gipsy-wort, *Lycopus europaeus,* and scull-cap, *Scutellaria galericulata,* appear on the "storm beaches" formed by wave action. The flora of the damper woods contains marsh marigold, *Caltha palustris;* lesser celandine, *Ranunculus ficaria;* marsh violet, *Viola palustris;* wood sorrel; marsh pennywort, *Hydrocotyle vulgaris;* bugle; yellow pimpernel, *Lysimachia nemorum;* and bog asphodel, *Narthecium ossifragum.* In the drier woods there are found the wood violet, *Viola sylvatica;* square-stalked St. John's-wort, *Hypericum tetrapterum;* foxglove, *Digitalis purpurea;* self-heal, *Prunella vulgaris;* wood-sage, *Teucrium scorodonia;* dog's mercury, *Mercurialis perennis;* orchids; wild hyacinth, *Endymion nutans;* and the hard fern, *Blechnum boreale.* Maiden-hair spleenwort, *Asplenium trichomanes,* wall-rue, *A. rutamuraria,* and brittle bladder fern, *Cystopteris fragilis,* appear on the walls and bridges.

The region south of Rowardennan is the happy hunting ground of mycologists, especially in those spots where, in the past, the saw-mill has been at work. In this area, too, most of the galls that grow on the oak may be found:—marble gall, oak spangles, oak apples (both stem and root galls) and the artichoke gall.

Space does not permit of a comparison with Loch Ard, Loch Chon, Loch Achray, Lochan Spling or Loch Drunkie. Each possesses an interesting flora.

THE RIVER VALLEYS

With the exception of those streams which enter Loch Lomond and so feed the River Leven and Firth of Clyde, the whole river system of the Forest Park belongs to the Forth drainage area. In their lower reaches the streams are usually sluggish. The Allt a Mhangan, which flows south through Aberfoyle, rises near the slate quarries north-west of Craigmore. Before it reaches Aberfoyle it has cut a deep gorge possessing many picturesque waterfalls. The gorge is rich in mosses and liverworts. The streamside is densely wooded, chiefly with birches, hazels and willows. Blackthorns, *Prunus spinosa,* make the going difficult. On the slopes above the burn an occasional plant of ling or heather has been found with some of its branches bearing white flowers, the others, purple flowers.

An outstanding feature of the Duchray Water and the Laggan is the sombre junipers which stand out strongly against the other vegetation.

Before the Kelty Water reaches the Drymen–Gartmore road, on its way to Flanders Moss, it passes through a heather-moorland which bears greater bird's foot trefoil, *Lotus major;* marsh cinque-foil, *Potentilla palustre;* cross-leaved heath, *Erica tetralix;* bog myrtle, *Myrica gale;* bog asphodel; jointed rush, *Juncus articulatus;* deer's hair, *Scirpus caespitosus;* beak rush, *Rynchospora alba;* and a wealth of orchids, e.g., lesser and greater butterfly, *Platanthera bifolia* and *P. chlorantha;* fragrant, *Gymnadenia conopsea;* early purple, and spotted, *Orchis mascula* and *O. maculata.* The hazels of this region produce abundant and excellent nuts.

HEATHS AND MOORLANDS

Mention has already been made of the bracken and heath zones; the greater part of the Forest Park lies within these. Boulder clay or till reaches high up on to the hills. Back through the ages vegetation has added its quota of humus to the soil. Thus, representatives of several of the types of heath and moor are to be found in the area. The drier humose soils give the *Calluna* Heath and the drier peats the *Calluna* Moor. The deep wet peat produces the *Eriophorum* Moor with bog cotton, *Eriophorum* spp., deer's-hair grass, and sphagnum dominant. Finally, there is the Grass Moor where the dominant plants are purple moor-grass, *Molinia caerulea;* heath rush, *Juncus squarrosus;* and mat grass, *Nardus stricta.*

The area contains several rare plants. These should be allowed to remain in their natural habitat. Even the less rare should not be uprooted. In fact, some naturalists consider that a "herbarium" of plant photographs is more to be desired than a "cemetery" of dried specimens. The botanist in pursuit of his field work does not neglect the scenery; and, such surroundings as he will have in this Forest Park cannot fail to make this pursuit more enjoyable.

*   *   *

Beneath the golden gloamin' sky
The mavis mends her lay;
The redbreast pours his sweetest strains
To charm the lingering day.

—Tannahill, *The Midges Dance Aboon the Burn.*

BIRD LIFE

By C. E. Palmar

From the point of view of a field ornithologist this Forest Park may be divided into five different habitats:

(1) Human habitations and their immediate environments.
(2) Loch, river, burn and marsh.
(3) Coniferous plantation.
(4) Hillside oak and birch scrub.
(5) Upland grass, moor, and mountain, above 500 feet.

Although these divisions are somewhat arbitrary they form, nevertheless, a practicable basis upon which the visitor may make his observations. The first habitat, scattered in small pockets where man has largely shaped the countryside, holds most of the usual birds, and a list will suffice. The following are either common, or at any rate not really unusual:

Rook, jackdaw, magpie, starling, greenfinch, linnet, chaffinch, yellow bunting, house-sparrow, pied wagtail (illustrated at the head of this chapter), tree-creeper, great tit, blue tit, coal tit, long-tailed tit, spotted flycatcher, goldcrest, willow-warbler, garden-warbler, blackcap, whitethroat, fieldfare, mistle-thrush, song-thrush, redwing, blackbird, robin, hedgesparrow, wren, swallow, house-martin, sand-martin, swift, great spotted woodpecker, cuckoo, long-eared owl, tawny owl, barn owl, kestrel, sparrow-hawk, wood-pigeon, stock-dove, lapwing, gulls of the black-headed, common, herring, lesser black-backed and greater black-backed species; corncrake, moorhen, pheasant and partridge.

With the exception of the fieldfare and redwing, which are winter visitors, and the possible exception of the swift, corncrake, rook and sand-martin, these species can be regarded as breeding regularly within the park (or perhaps within a stone's-throw of its boundaries, as with the gulls on the Loch Lomond islands).

Small patches of marshy ground are often found, especially around the lochs—and the appropriate common species are present: reed-bunting, meadow-pipit, sedge-warbler, mallard, teal, wigeon, snipe, lapwing and moorhen; all nest except the wigeon.

Naturally, with so many lochs on the edges of the Park, and several lochans within it, there is a good variety of water-fowl: to the three ducks already named may be added shoveller, pochard, tufted duck, goldeneye, goosander and merganser, although conditions are not suitable for any really large regular winter concentrations of fowl such as at the Endrick mouth, and on the Lake of Menteith. Other visitors to the waters are the whooper swan, mute swan, cormorant, great crested grebe, little grebe, all three divers, common and arctic terns, the five gulls already named, moorhen and coot. To the shores of the lochs and rivers come the common sandpiper, redshank, oystercatcher and heron, whilst the larger burns form suitable haunts for the dipper and grey wagtail. An occasional kingfisher may be seen where the rivers are not too swift, or by the loch sides. Greylag geese pass overhead occasionally, but have no regular resting-place in the Park.

We come now to what, from the point of view of the student of ecology, is the most interesting habitat of all—the coniferous plantation. Any given planting may not, in itself, appear of particular interest, but if ones of various ages are compared, an absorbing picture of how man can change an environment appears.

First of all, the unplanted hillside will have a bird population in which the meadow-pipit is the dominant breeding species. There are also skylarks, curlews, and perhaps wheatears, stonechats and reed buntings. When planting begins the ground is fenced off, and with sheep and deer excluded, the ungrazed grass grows thickly, forming excellent cover for mice and voles, which increase rapidly. This brings about an increase of creatures which prey upon them, such as stoats, weasels, kestrels, buzzards and short-eared owls.

These owls begin to breed amongst the young trees and thick grass. As this vegetation grows the wheatears, meadow-pipits, skylarks and curlews disappear, and the dominant breeding species becomes the willow-warbler—hitherto perhaps quite absent. Whinchats, black-game and robins also breed at this stage, but the former disappear when the trees get about five feet high, and begin to stifle the grass. The rodent population now declines, along with its attendant short-eared owls and kestrels. New species take their place—such birds as chaffinches, bullfinches, greenfinches, linnets, lesser redpolls, goldcrests and tits—including the long-tailed tit. The willow-warbler hangs on for good—but passes its peak numbers when the trees are around five feet in height.

This population is fairly stable until the trees reach a height around twelve feet, when carrion crows, wood-pigeons, and perhaps jays, arrive; goldcrests, tits and chaffinches maintain their numbers, but the other finches tend to decrease. At this stage, if red or grey squirrels appear they form a limiting factor in the small bird population, as they are destructive to nests and eggs. When the trees get to the twenty-foot stage, the long-eared owl finds them an eminently suitable sanctuary, and the great spotted woodpecker arrives. Finally crossbills and capercaillies frequent fully mature plantations, though this is a recent development as far as Loch Ard is concerned. At the moment the crossbill is an occassional visitor, and the "caper" apparently nested for the first time in 1951—although it has nested outside the Park for many years. The transformation from bare hillside to mature forest over the years is thus a most absorbing one. The foregoing is, of course, only a broad outline.

The natural oak and birch scrub, with which is often associated rowan, hazel and alder, which clothes the lower hillside in many places, is by far the richest bird-haunt of all. It is here that the gaudy coloured jay (a curiously local bird in Scotland) finds a suitable home; likewise, those two other avian rogues, the hooded crow and carrion crow, whose breeding ranges meet roughly at the Highland Boundary Fault, nest, and not infrequently interbreed. Hybrids are not uncommon. Among the finches, chaffinch, bullfinch, green-finch, and lesser redpoll are well represented, whilst the tree-creeper finds the old gnarled bark much to his liking. In summer-time the tree-pipit mounts into the air and "parachutes" down to the top of a tree, singing persistently awhile; it nests on the ground amongst open spaces. The three "leaf-warblers" are present—the willow-warbler in strength, the wood warbler only locally, and the chiff-chaff in small numbers only. Garden-warbler and whitethroat are other summer denizens in limited numbers—though the last named is common enough locally, especially in brambles and whin. The grasshopper-warbler has been heard around Lochan Spling, and may perhaps breed in the spring.

Amongst the tit fraternity, the coal tit is probably the most numerous, and the long-tailed the least so; the blue tit and the great tit are universal amongst the trees, as are the thrushes—song-thrush mistle-thrush and blackbird—and the familiar robin, wren and hedge-sparrow. Two noteworthy summer visitors are the redstart—that delightful little bird whose red tail and underparts flash in the sun as he flits from tree to tree—and the cuckoo, which lays in the nests of robin and hedge-sparrow in the woods, or meadow-pipit on the open hillside hard by. The great spotted woodpecker loves the oaks and birches, often using a dead stump of the latter tree for excavating its nesting hole.

Four predators of these hillside scrub-woods are the tawny owl, kestrel, buzzard and sparrow-hawk—the first three almost entirely beneficial birds. Wood-pigeon and stock-dove are found—the former not, however, in such great numbers as in the plantations. Woodcock and pheasant are reasonably common nesters on the ground (the former being particularly hard to find) whilst the blackcock (or rather his greyhen mate) prefers a spot where the trees meet the heather for its abode.

This scrub extends upwards to round about 500 feet and perhaps to 700 feet in places up the burns; above this—and often well below it—the coarse grass, sphagnum, and heather of the mountainsides begins in earnest. Many of the small birds such as robins, wrens, hedge-sparrows and reed-buntings extend to—and even nest in—this sphere, even up to 1,500 feet; whilst the ubiquitous meadow-pipits and wheatears know no limit, being found on the summit of Ben Lomond itself.

The ring ousel, or mountain blackbird, is occasionally found around 1,500 feet; the cock bird (whose white crescent on the breast is more conspicuous than that of his spouse) claims attention with his loud fluting whistling song, or angry *"chak"* of alarm—both often given from a crag. Amongst the heather we would expect the twite, or mountain linnet; the cock has a red-coloured rump. But I have yet to see one on the Park's moorlands. The cuckoo may call even from around the 1,500 foot contour; so may the skylark still soar on high.

The wide rolling moors form the home *par excellence* of the red grouse (whose existence is virtually inseparable from the ling upon which it mainly feeds) and also, in places, of the black grouse; the short-eared owl, too, floats above it by day—like some huge diurnal moth. In the right sort of place—perhaps some windswept ridge where the heather is short—the magic skirling of that most beautiful bird, the golden plover, comes floating down the breeze. Maybe you will nearly tread on his hen-bird as she crouches, perfectly camouflaged, over her four pear-shaped eggs amongst the moorland herbage in the month of May.

But *the* "wading" bird of the moors and mountains is, of course, the whaup or curlew, whose ecstatic, bubbling love-calls, or plaintive anxiety-notes after which he is named, may be heard almost anywhere in the Park. So, too, may the far less welcome notes of the five common species of gulls, which, from their bases on the waters and islets of Loch Lomond, range far and wide over the hills, ever on the lookout for pickings of any kind. Even more expert as a scrounger is the much-hated hooded crow, a handsome rogue found right up to the tops. The dainty merlin—the ladies' falcon—nests sparingly amongst the heather, whilst the golden eagle, hen-harrier and snow-bunting are occasional non-breeding visitors to these high moors.

Next come the two crag-nesters—raven and peregrine; noble birds both of them, especially when, on the wing, they tilt at each other in aerial combat. Both nest within the Park. Last of all is the ptarmigan, that curious bird of three plumages to the year, of which the winter one is pure white, like the snow amongst which it then lives. The Park lies at the southernmost limit of this bird's range in Great Britain, for it is found around 3,000 feet on Ben Lomond.

It will be seen that, although the boundaries of the Park have been closely adhered to when writing the foregoing, the area covered, containing highland, marginal and lowland ground, is appropriately rich in bird life.

* * *

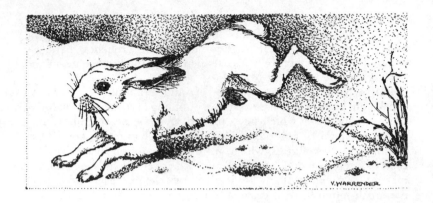

As for the little growling doe
And her young fawns who bide
In a hidden glen ill to know
High up the mountain side,
The ear she has! And the eye!
And the quick deft feet to ply
Over the boggling peat-hags!
Lightning behind her lags.

—Duncan Ban MacIntyre, *In Praise of Beinn Dorain.*

THE MAMMALS OF THE PARK

By C. E. Palmar

The diverse nature of the Park, with its natural woods, thick plantations, heather clad moors, high mountains and a generous system of waters gives it a wide mammalian fauna, ranging from the pigmy shrew to the red deer—our smallest and our largest mammals respectively.

Amongst the insectivora, the mole, the hedgehog and the three shrews—common, pigmy and water, are widely distributed. When the snow lies on the ground one realises what an active creature the mole is, for the fresh, unfrozen mounds of newly-upraised earth give an index of the energy of this little miner which, with his sensitive snout, spade-like claws, and fur with hairs coming out perpendicularly, is so perfectly equipped for an underground livelihood. The mole is found several hundred feet up the hillside. Its main sustenance is earthworms.

Worms, too, are an important item with the hedgehog—but its diet is really omnivorous. It is one of the few enemies of the adder, which strikes against its quills and eventually so damages itself that the "hedgepig" uncurls, runs in quickly and bites the snake through the backbone. Hedgehogs probably hibernate more regularly and deeply in the Loch Ard area than on the milder coastal area of the west.

Bats are quite frequently seen, especially beside the lochs, but I have never managed to identify any of the species myself as they pass on the wing. The common bat or pipistrelle is recorded as living up to its adjectival name; unquestionably others are present.

Carnivorous beasts are present in smaller numbers than one might reasonably expect, for with the exellent cover afforded by the thick plantations, foxes, stoats, weasels and wild cats would increase very rapidly but for the efforts of the Commission's Rangers. As a matter of fact, these creatures prey heavily on the rodent population, which can play havoc with young trees, and in this way they are the foresters' friends; however, the Commission very rightly considers the position of the local farmers, and keeps the carnivores in check.

Stoats, which often turn white in winter, can always be told from weasels as the latter animals lack the black tip to the tail. The wild cat is probably the most interesting of the carnivores of the Park. Here it virtually reaches the southernmost limit of its range, and only a few are seen each year. Its numbers are unlikely to become great. It will not take dead bait in a trap, as do escaped domestic cats.

Badgers are found in the Park, but they are few in number. Otters, on the other hand, are more common; the rivers and lochs are very suitable for them. It is, however, a mistake to imagine that they are tied to water; they habitually travel far from it overland.

Perhaps the day may not be far off when the forests will once more hold a limited number of pine martens. Those beautiful orange-throated members of the Mustelidae, although quite understandably unwelcome in many quarters, would be an exciting addition to the Park's fauna. Odd specimens of this animal, the natural enemy of the squirrels, which it chases from branch to branch amongst the tree-tops, have occurred in the Commission's forests elsewhere. But the polecat has apparently gone for good (do any still exist in Scotland?) and few would wish this bloodthirsty creature, the ancestor of the ferret, back again.

The rodent population is, as usual, by far the most numerous. A ceaseless war is waged against rabbits, brown hares, and mountain hares, which are controlled as far as possible within the fenced-off plantations. The last-named animal, which is found on Ben Lomond

39

and other high mountains, turns almost pure white in winter, as shown in the drawing which heads this chapter. The brown hare is most partial to the cultivated areas.

The bank-vole and the short-tailed field-vole are probably both plentiful, but I cannot claim to have given them much attention. The much larger, more conspicuous and much more interesting and observable water vole is found where the waters are not too rapid. It lives in holes in the banks, and is often persecuted because of the implications of its unfortunate common name of "water-rat". In point of fact it eats aquatic vegetable matter, and may often be seen licking itself carefully as, engrossed in its toilet, it sits on a flat platform of nibbled-off reeds or horse-tails. A melanistic specimen from Aberfoyle is in the Glasgow Museum at Kelvingrove.

The long-tailed field mouse, the house mouse and the brown rat are naturally present in the Park, and as unwelcome as they are elsewhere. Red squirrels are not too plentiful. Grey squirrels are chiefly found on the Loch Lomond shores; any extension of range and numbers would be most unwelcome in the forests. One cannot help wondering if this virile, introduced American species would have spread so rapidly in so many parts of England, and be doing the enormous damage reported, if a suitable natural predator in the shape of the pine marten had still existed there to deal with it. Fortunately its numbers in Scotland are by no means so serious, and its range is limited, at least so far, to the Lowlands.

Amongst the hoofed animals the red deer, roe deer and fallow deer are found. The former exists in reasonable numbers on the higher ground, but the much smaller roe is a forest animal; it is not uncommon. Since fallow deer are found on the western shores of Loch Lomond, and on some islands, a few can probably be seen on the east side of the loch. But if this is so, they do not appear to have strayed over the hills to the Aberfoyle region. Herds of "wild" goats are to be seen on the slopes of Ben Lomond, and also on Cruinn a Bheinn.

AMPHIBIANS AND REPTILES

Frogs and toads are quite common in most places in the Park. I have seen the former amazingly high up in the hills—around 1,500 feet or so, and they have both been recorded well over 2,000 feet!

The smooth newt, palmate newt and crested newt have all been recorded from the Aberfoyle area, but I am unaware as to their precise status.

The common lizard is the commonest of the three reptiles present; it can often be seen sunning itself on roadside banks, or among

Plate 26. Pony trekkers at Aberfoyle.

Plate 27. A load of timber crosses Aberfoyle Bridge on its way to the sawmill.

Plate 28. Loch Drunkie. The eastward view from the Duke's Road down the Teith valley towards Callander.

Plate 29. Fringed by alders and oaks, the Forth winds beneath the old bridge at Aberfoyle.

Plate 30.   Loch Katrine's winding shores, seen from the summit of Ben A'an, looking west towards the Arrochar peaks.

Plate 31.   The Loch Katrine steamer *Sir Walter Scott* leaving the pier at Stronachlachar.

Plate 32. The David Marshall Lodge, on the hilltop overlooking Aberfoyle.

Plate 33. Playbreak at Inversnaid School, which draws scholars of varied ages from the scattered homesteads around.

Plate 34.   Cobleland Camp Site, beside the Forth near Aberfoyle.

Plate 35.   Ben Venue towers above the rocky shores of Loch Katrine, clad in birches, oaks and pines.

Plate 36. The view from the Duke's Road over the David Marshall Lodge and Flanders Moss to the Campsie Fells.

Plate 37. Looking across Loch Chon towards Frenich Farm and the plantations of Loch Ard Forest, between Aberfoyle and Stronachlachar.

the heather—even well up into the hills. The slow-worm or blind-worm—which is neither slow, blind, nor a worm—is the least common of the reptiles. This most interesting creature is a legless lizard. It has the power of shedding its tail in order to escape when caught, or even alarmed.

Finally comes an object of the utmost revulsion, and horror verging on terror . . . . or a charming, extremely beautiful and fascinating creature—according to one's psychological make-up; thus is the adder variously regarded. It is quite common in many parts of the Park, and emerges from hibernation early in April, if in fact, not sooner. It should not be handled on any account.

I should like to acknowledge generous assistance in confirming certain points, and in amplifying others, from the Forestry Commision staff at Aberfoyle.

*　　*　　*

These waters move as they have moved alway
In solitude beneath the splintered hills,
The bent and heather browse upon their spray,
And curlews toss their light on golden bills.
Imponderable beams at noon of day
Are baulked against the ethiopic deeps
Wherein cold eels scare minnows from their play,
Whereunder rock,⸀the earth's foundation, sleeps.

—William Jeffrey, *Loch Sloy.*

THE STRUCTURE
AND FRESHWATER BIOLOGY
OF LOCH LOMOND

By Dr. H. D. Slack

Largest of British lakes in area, Loch Lomond covers 27.45 square miles, and contains about 93,000 million cubic feet of water. Two-thirds of this water mass lies below sea-level in a deep valley gouged out of Dalradian rock by a glacier in the Ice Age. The main dynamic factors which gave the loch its form were the grinding action of this glacier, together with the vertical movement of the land during and after the glaciation; a movement which submerged the lower part of the loch below the sea and finally raised its surface some thirty feet above sea-level. Moraine and marine deposits from ice and sea have given this part its low-lying sand and gravel shores and relatively wide water body; in strong contrast to the steep rock shores of the deep and narrow upper loch where it lies confined by encroaching hills.

The geological structure and history of the region have played their part not only in the shaping of the loch but also, by determining the nature of its bottom deposits and the chemical constitution of its waters, have defined the habitats of its plants and animals. The Highland Boundary Fault, crossing from Balmaha to Arden through the line of islands—Inchcailloch, Torrinch, Creinch and Inchmurrin, is a convenient starting point for a brief survey of the four main geological regions because they were formed primarily by its agency. South of these islands the loch lies on Lower Old Red Sandstone. North of them, sandstone of the Highland Boundary Series traverses the loch where lie three low flat islands; Inchfad, Inchcruin and Inchmoan. North of these again the remaining major islands, Inchtavanach, Inchconachan, Buccinch and Inchlonaig, rise in the first of the Dalradian rocks exposed by erosion after up-thrust when the fault was formed. These rocks extend northwards to Ross Point where they give way to the older and more highly metamorphosed formations underlying the upper half of the loch. In the latter, the glacier excavated the deepest basins, one reaching a maximum depth of 623 feet near Inversnaid.

Throughout the centuries that have followed the initial shaping of the loch, inflowing steams and waves generated by the winds have altered the character of its marginal waters. Streams flowing into the loch are numerous, but for the most part are small burns. Only the larger ones have formed deltas about their mouths; notably the rivers Falloch, Endrick and Fruin; the last two, flowing mainly over softer formations, carry greater quantities of mineral sediments into the lower part of the loch.

The increased breadth of the lower loch, its easily eroded alluvial shores, and open nature of the surrounding country have all combined to facilitate the action of waves in cutting back the shores and transporting material from them into the loch, to form wide terraces sloping gently down to the deeper water. These terraces vary with the nature of the shore; fine gravels grading to sands and silts in the alluvial regions, or starting with an outer zone of stones where the more resistant Old Red Sandstone conglomerates occur.

Such terracing in the upper loch is entirely different. Here it takes the form of a narrower, deeper shelf cut in the sides of the glacial trough and falling steeply for a hundred feet or more to the profundal loch bed.

Since the major part of the water-shed lies in Pre-Cambrian country, the water of the loch is soft, has a low mineral content and a moderately high transparency.

With the passage of time the loch bed has received a steady accumulation of the remains of plants and animals; much of it in the form of branches and leaves from the trees which clothe its shores and climb the glens of the water-shed. Finally reduced to a fine brown mud this organic material settles to the bottom, there to form the humus of the aquatic soils; some to be buried and some ultimately to form the food of plants and animals.

Having set the scene it is now possible to see what living organisms have availed themselves of conditions for life in this little world below the surface of the water. It is in a sense an inverted world with vegetation on the high ground and a monotonous waste of bare mud on the low.

Green plants must have a certain intensity of light for the process of photosynthesis in order to survive, and light intensity falls rapidly with increasing water depth. Therefore green plants which are attached to or rooted in the sub-strata can only extend from the shore to where the water is about twelve feet deep.

Consequently their principal development is on the wide terraces of the lower loch. Here the type of bottom deposit and concomitant degree of wave disturbance determines the species distribution. On the marginal stones swept by breaking water no macrophytes survive other than clumps of such a moss as *Fontinalis antepyretica*. Further out where sand and gravel has settled, lake-wort, *Littorella uniflora* Asch., forms a close-set sward binding and stabilising the bottom. In the same zone the pale blue flowers of water lobelia, *Lobelia dortmanna* L., emerge in summer where the water is sufficiently shallow. Beyond the lake-wort a similar sward of quill-wort, *Isoetes lacustris* L., takes its place, to be succeeded on the finer sands, and in quieter water, by water milfoil, *Myriophyllum spicatum* L., and the alga, *Nitella opaca*.

With increasing deposition of organic muds as the water deepens, species of pondweed appear, such as *Potamogeton perfoliatus* and *P. praelongus*. It is only in a few very sheltered regions affording a pond-like habitat that pondweed of the *P. natans* type occurs. *P. polygonifolius* is such a species, and with it are to be found water starwort, *Callitriche intermedia*, and *Scirpus fluitans*. Likewise restricted to sheltered places are such plants as *Scirpus lacustris*, reeds, *Phragmites*, and horsetails, *Equisetum*. In the shelter of "The Narrows" between the islands of Inchtavanach and Inchconachan, even the yellow water lily, *Nuphar luteum*, holds its own. Elsewhere in the neighbourhood it is found only in small tarns, Lochan Geal at the head of the loch, and the Dubh Lochan near Rowardennan.

As with the plants so with the animals. It is on the shallow wave-cut terraces and on such submerged banks as the Rossdhu and Macdougal Banks, that invertebrate animals living on the bottom reach their greatest numbers and variety of species. Con-

44

sequently these regions are also the principal feeding grounds of most of the fishes and of the waterfowl.

The stony or gravelly margins close in-shore, periodically exposed at low water and, when covered, subjected to strong wave-wash during on-shore winds, are sparsely populated. With the establishment of the *Littorella* and *Isoetes* swards come more stable conditions, and a rich growth of epiphytic algae as a source of food. Both in numbers and species the fauna is greatly augmented, not only by lacustrine types but also by some of those to be found in the neighbouring burns; for currents of sufficient frequency and velocity provide a satisfactory environment. Here live the nymphs of some ten species of mayfly, including the sand-burrowing *Ephemera danica;* the larvae of at least thirty species of caddis-fly and of many species of chironomid midges; aquatic bugs, beetles and mites; the water skater, *Asellus aquaticus;* several genera of water snails and the pea-shells, *Sphaerium* and *Pisidium;* aquatic earthworms such as *Eisseniella* and *Lumbriculus,* together with many other forms.

This fauna changes as the water deepens and the bottom sediments become finer, in favour of those animals preferring still waters. For example such caddis-flies appear as *Phrygania varia* and *Limnophilus rhombicus,* whose larval cases are large but too lightly built to withstand the wash of waves.

In the outermost zone of green plants the bottom mud is usually too soft for caddis-flies and mayflies, except the tiny *Caenis horaria.* Worms, chironomid midge larvae and *Pisidium* predominate, and finally, in the deep waters off-shore where no green plants can survive, these animals are almost the only ones to find a living in the soft organic mud.

A second community of plants and animals has no direct dependence upon the loch bed. This is the plankton, a congregation of minute animals living upon equally minute plants which drift through all the upper layers of water where enough light penetrates for their survival. The characteristic planktonic plants are such diatoms as *Asterionella formosa* and *Tabellaria fenestrarara* var. *asterionelloides,* and such desmids as *Staurastrum* species. Their abundance in the spring is great enough to change the colour of the water to a browner shade. In the summer blue-green algae predominate, especially *Coelosphaerium* species. This occasionally drifts to the shores as a green scum, but Loch Lomond never produces the dense "water-bloom" that blue-green algae form in lakes with waters rich in nutritive salts.

The animals of the plankton are composed of several groups. Those visible to the naked eye as bright specks in the water on a sunny day, belong to crustacean orders popularly called "water fleas". The most numerous are *Daphnia hyalina, Bosmina obtusirostris,*

45

Diaptomus gracilis and species of *Cyclops*. Preying on them are their much larger and more active relatives, *Leptodora kindtii* and *Bythotrephes longimannus*.

The beautiful cladoceran, *Holopedium gibberum*, is abundant in the quieter waters of the Dubh Lochan, but is too delicate a creature to flourish in the larger lochs.

Loch bed and open water with their myriads of inhabitants are the pastures and hunting grounds of fishes and birds.

Loch Lomond has a high repute among anglers for the salmon and sea-trout which pass through on their way from the sea to breed in rivers and burns. Brown trout and pike range the inshore waters. Perch, roach, minnows and three- and nine-spined sticklebacks abound, especially on the richer feeding grounds of the lower loch. All the British species of lamprey occur, and one, at least, is a serious pest to fishes. *Petromyzon marinus* comes from the sea to spawn while *P. fluviatilis* and the smaller *Lampetra planeri* appear to be resident.

The most notable fish is that illustrated at the head of this chapter, namely the powan, *Coregonus clupeoides*, for this fish is found only in Loch Lomond and Loch Eck. Once a marine fish it adapted itself to freshwater when the rising land at the end of the Ice Age isolated it from the sea. More than all the others it turned to that abundant source of food—the plankton. Today it is probably the most abundant species in the loch.

The resident water birds most frequently to be seen on the loch are the red-breasted merganser, the mallard and the cormorant, but others, less often seen, such as the sheld-duck, have become established breeding species. Gulls frequent it at all times, especially the black-headed gull, while each summer sees the return of common and black-headed terns to nest on one of the islands, and the common sandpiper on the shores. In the early morning or at dusk in calm summer weather the heron stands on watch for fish in the shallows.

A pair of mute swans are usually to be seen, but the whooper swan only as a winter visitor. Geese, especially the pink-footed goose, come regularly to the loch in winter, and this season sees the arrival of many ducks—wigeon, pochard, scaup duck and golden-eye. Severe winters bring rarer visitors. Both the red-throated diver and the red-necked grebe were found dead in 1947, having unfortunately failed to survive when ice covered all the lower part of the loch.

The smaller lochs and lochans have a fauna and flora that is broadly similar to that of Loch Lomond, but space does not permit of detailed descriptions here. As a rule, they tend to be richer in those forms of life that require still water, as the amount of wave action increases with the size of the loch.

46

Aloft, the ash and warrior oak
Cast anchor in the rifted rock;
And, higher yet, the pine-tree hung
His shatter'd trunk, and frequent flung,
Where seem'd the cliffs to meet on high,
His boughs athwart the narrow'd sky.

—Scott, *The Lady of the Lake:*

FORESTRY

By J. E. James and Roger Hurst

THE SETTING

FORESTRY in this district is not a new occupation or use for the land. From the *Statistical Account* of 1794 planned forestry was being practised in the main valley of Loch Chon and Loch Ard to yield material useful to the countryside and provide employment. The locality was then described as a land of lakes bordered by woodlands of oak, ash and birch. These woodlands ran to halfway up the mountain slopes with the lower hills wooded right to their summits. Doon Hill near Aberfoyle, known also as the Fairy Knowe, was entirely covered with oaks as it is today. The woods were managed to a well planned programme, being divided into twenty-four parcels of equal extent, each an annual felling area. Today we describe this as a "coppice-with-standards" system and even in 1794 there were regulations to ensure adequate restocking with

47

standard trees. Forest products were then oak bark for the extraction of tannin, building and fencing materials, and wood for fuel.

From the *Second Statistical Account* of 1845 it is evident that the same planned forestry was continuing with emphasis on the enclosure of the annual cutting area to facilitate its regeneration. It is also mentioned that intermediate thinnings of the crops were practised.

Though the Forestry Commission was formed in 1919 no land was acquired here until 1928 when 4,000 acres (1,620 hectares) were purchased immediately south of Loch Ard. At this time the agriculture of the locality was suffering depression, aggravated by the virtual collapse of stock-rearing due to tick- and fluke-borne diseases, and land acquisition continued until by 1945 some 27,000 acres (10,930 hectares) had been acquired. Post war acquisitions occured mainly during the 1950's, giving the following situation in 1972.

Forest	Acres	Hectares	Square Miles
Loch Ard Forest	23,517	9,517	36.8
Achray Forest	8,866	3,588	13.8
Rowardennan (part of Buchanan Forest)	9,590	3,881	15.0
Queen Elizabeth Forest Park: Total	41,973	16,986	65.6

The Forest Park is thus approximately 65 square miles in a fairly compact block, but within it there are varieties of site types which are of great importance in the treatment of land. From the chapter on Geology it will be seen that the Park spans the Highland Boundary Fault which itself separates the Old Red Sandstone to the south from the Dalradian rocks to the north. Superimposed over this are the glacial effects, mainly the deposition of boulder clay over the Old Red Sandstone and irregular mound-like gravel moraines over the less steep parts of the Dalradian Series. Geology and topography, together with the influences of climate and previous land use, have given rise to the major soil types. The richer lower ground consists of the more fertile Brown Forest Soils, while on the intermediate hill slopes the gravelly soils of the humpy moraines protrude out of a matrix of poorly-drained mineral soils, finally rising into the hill peats of the higher slopes up to the limit of the forest land at an altitude of about 1,200 feet above sea level. To put the soils of the forest within perspective their proportions are as follows:—

Well drained mineral soils: 25% Brown Forest soils and Iron Pan soils
Poorly drained mineral soils: 50% Gleyed soils
Peats: 25% Hill peats

48

The forester must know the soils of his forest as these influence the type of ground cultivation, the intensity of drainage that should be imposed, the nutrient deficiencies which have to be corrected by the application of fertilizer, etc. These not only influence the choice of species that he should plant, but can have effects on work programmes throughout the life of the tree crop. Impeded drainage for example can have a critical influence on stability of forty-foot high trees in high winds.

The different types of ground vegetation must also be investigated as these not only give a clue to the soil types but do themselves influence of the forest work programmes especially when the trees are small and need weeding. Dead vegetation in the late winter period is also a major factor in the hazard of forest fires starting easily and spreading fast. Finally the forester must take account of the climatic factors as they also influence his work planning in many respects, from the number of wet days on which work cannot proceed, to whether long-lying snow prevents the timber lorries gaining access to the timber stacks. A strong gale in April 1967 brought down some 18,000 cubic metres (roughly 18,000 tons) of timber but this was only in the form of a dress rehersal for the major hurricane of January 1968 which flattened some 2½ square miles of forest bringing down a further 75,000 cubic metres. The effects of this hurricane will be evident in the forests around Aberfoyle and the Trossachs for many years to come.

To continue the work of creating and maintaining the forests of the Park, the Commission employs in the locality some 120 staff, which includes seven women, mainly clerical staff. To house its staff the Commission owns over a hundred houses within the Park. Not all the work in the forests is done by the Commission's employees, for timber is also worked by timber merchants who regularly have a further fifteen men employed for this purpose.

MANAGING THE FORESTS

FORMATION OF NEW PLANTATIONS

MUCH of the land is covered to a varying depth by peat which does not allow a wide choice of variety of tree species. The peat areas in the first years were dealt with by hand draining, the turf from the drains being spread at intervals over the land and the young trees, chiefly spruces, planted into the upturned turves. This system gave good results and spruces were found to start growth almost immediately without check. Later on in 1938 this form of cultivation was mechanised with wide-tracked crawler tractors and heavy drainage ploughs, and it is this method which has been further developed and is used today, with the plough turning out ribbons of upturned thick turf from a deep furrow. On the firmer mineral soils heavier tractors with normal-width tracks can be used and the plough can have a long tine protruding below the furrow to break up iron-pans or compacted sub-soils. It is on these drier slopes that larches, Douglas fir and pines have been planted. As these sites are the ones most in the public eye it is fortunate from a landscaping point of view that such a variety of colour and texture of foliage is possible. The trees used are raised from seed in districts of lower rainfall; they are about three years old and nine inches tall when planted out, usually at six feet apart (See Plate 51). To date the proportion of tree species planted within the Park are as follows:—

Spruces:	65%	Sitka and Norway spruces
Pines:	15%	Scots and Lodgepole pines
Larches:	10%	Japanese larch
Other conifers:	5%	Douglas fir, Western hemlock and Silver fir
Broadleaves:	5%	Oak and beech

As the mechanisation of ploughing has taken much of the physical effort out of planting, so the application of fertilizers by helicopter or fixed-wing planes have eased the task of applying three hundred-weight of crushed Gafsa Rock Phosphate to each acre at the time of planting. (Plate 52). The soils derived from Dalriadan rocks are essentially deficient in phosphate. This situation was not improved by the high rainfall nor by the previous history of sheep grazing, which led to phosphorus leaving the land in the fleeces and bodies of the sheep, with no return through fertilising.

Either before, or within five years of planting, a system of deep cross drains is superimposed through the planting land. These are from two to three feet deep and their intensity is dictated by the type of site because the object is to provide a deep rooting medium to give the crop stability against gales at a latter date.

On the lower more fertile ground and in bracken patches it is necessary to remove the competing weeds from around the young trees. Formerly this weeding would be done by hand using sickles to cut the weeds and this is still done where there is bracken. For other weeds the modern development of various selective weed-killers has permitted weed control by chemical means.

Until the 1968 hurricane virtually all the planting had taken place on bare ground not previously carrying a tree crop, but as the 2½ square miles which were blown flat have been cleared they have been speedily replanted. As the young trees planted through the debris are vulnerable to harmful beetles breeding in the old stumps, they are dipped in an insecticide before planting.

50

Fences are not put around each year's plantings but are planned for the forest overall and the pre-requisite of such a plan is to determine what the trees require protection from. Where this is from sheep or cattle then the type and location of such fences can be determined by liaison with farm neighbours. Rabbits, hares and roe deer can all do damage to young trees but their numbers within the Park are such that it is more economical to control their populations to levels which can live adequately off the food supplies within the forest, without damaging the trees. This is much more practical and cheaper than fencing specially against these animals. To effect this control trained Forest Rangers are employed.

This leaves the wild goats of Ben Lomond and red deer, both very wide-ranging beasts not tied to restricted territories. Therefore the traditional six-foot high deer fence is maintained along the top boundaries of plantations adjacent to the land they frequent. Within the Forest Park there are quite substantial areas of land above the upper limit of the plantations to which the visitor has access, as on Ben Lomond and Ben Venue. These uplands all carry populations of wild red deer.

In the period January-June the dead ground vegetation, especially grass and bracken, will ignite easily on a dry sunny day if a visitor is careless with matches, cigarettes, picnic stoves, etc. A major outbreak of fire can build up rapidly under these conditions. To avoid this, visitors are requested to protect their forests by:—

Reporting any outbreak of fire to the fire brigade.

Using the fire brooms or beaters to put out ground fires.

Trying to persuade less thoughtful visitors not to continue with dangerous practices.

Parking vehicles so as to cause no obstructions to fire-fighting vehicles at forest entrances.

Giving way to fire-fighting vehicles.

Finally please use your car ashtrays.

HARVESTING AND MARKETING TIMBER

THE branches of the trees, originally planted fairly close together, join to form a dense thicket and rapid height growth then follows. To ensure that the best trees are allowed room to develop, both in height and girth, it is necessary to thin them out by removing the competing trees of inferior form. Thinnings usually commence when the plantations reach 20-25 years of age and continue at five-year intervals until the clear felling when the trees are around 50 years old. At a thinning approximately twenty tons of timber are removed from each acre of plantations. Both the start of thinning and date of clear felling is determined by the timber yielding capacity of the site, and the cultural regime applied throughout the life of the crop. Very basically timber is unsaleable when it is less than two inches (five centimetres) in diameter and there is not in this region, much demand for softwood logs with a diameter greater than twenty inches (fifty centimetres).

When the trees are reaching twenty years old the forester must consider what forest roads are to be built, and here he has to weigh the cost of building more roads closer together against the cost and method of moving the cut timber from the tree stump to the road-side. With road transport vehicles becoming larger and longer, and their gross weight increased, they require easier gradients, wider bends, stronger bridges and tougher surfacing than before. All this naturally increases the cost per mile of forest roads. Moving timber from stump to road is known as "extraction". Originally this was done by horses, but they have been superseded by winches which can pull in over 300 yards. This enables new roads to be placed at 600 yards apart, giving 2½–3 miles of road per square mile of forest, depending upon terrain.

The building of roads and bridges is the Forest Engineer's responsibility. His surveyors peg out the road-line on the ground, arranging with the forester to cut the trees in the path of the new road. Huge bulldozers or excavators cut out the formation, grade and surface to the correct camber and make provisions for passing places, stacking areas and turn-round points. Skilled workers with modern equipment drill and blast rock outcrops, cut side drains, lay culverts and make bridges. Then the tipper fleet moves in working from small quarries and gravel pits to add the surfacing stone which is finally graded and rolled. These roads wind and twist through the forest, following the lie of the land. Within the Park there are approximately one hundred miles of such roads which form such excellent walking routes that they are scarcely noticed for the good engineering works that they are in their own right.

The trees to be removed in thinnings are marked with a "blaze", a cut through the bark, by a small team who carry out, at the same time, a sampling system to estimate the volume of timber to be removed. One of their more difficult tasks is to mark straight lines called "extraction racks" to be cleared at intervals for the winch ropes. Following these markers comes the production team of five or six cutters who work spaced out into the forest from the road. Each man is self-contained with his light fast-cutting power saw, his belt to which are clipped maintenance tools and a spring loaded tape; not far away is his fuel and other equipment. He fells the tree, trims off the side branches, and cuts sawlogs and pulp with a precision and neatness borne of skill and experience (See Plates 53, 54 and 57).

Slightly further down the road, and seemingly hard on the cutters, is the winch, mounted on a tractor that often blocks the road itself. From its high tower winch ropes disappear into the plantations along the narrow rack. Alongside the winch stands the versatile winchman. His two hands operate four handles—a clutch and a brake to each of two winch drums. He keeps one foot on the accelerator pedal and his attention is directed down the rack to pick out signals from his "chokerman" (Plate 55). If the two men are working out of sight of each other, he listens to instructions by radio. The chokerman, deep in the wood (Plate 56), prepares the load of timber and hooks it into the carriage. After the load has been drawn in the winchman unhooks it at the roadside stack.

Lorries are now loaded by a hydraulic grab manipulated by one man who is often also the lorry driver (Plate 58). Because timber is sold at the forest roadside, the different stacks give a clue to the purchasers' requirements, either by tree species or specification. As loads are rarely of mixed products the lorries will be clearing timber from their own stacks. These may be short lengths of narrow diameter timber for the paper pulpmill at Fort William, or medium-diameter logs for boxwood, pit-props, pallet boards for fork-lift trucks, wood wool, etc. The biggest diameters and longest lengths are destined for sawmills which make a whole range of timber products, suitable for building or packaging.

LANDSCAPE AND RECREATION
SCENERY
The scenery of this Forest Park has a beauty of its own with a variety of form, texture and colour. The southern part has more gentle smoother slopes whilst in the north and west the peaks are higher and the slopes steeper with rocky outcrops. The valleys contain the most striking feature of the district—the Lochs. This topography arises of course from the geological history of the locality, but the site-type variation provides the intricate detail which plays so large a part in forming the scenic effect. Of these details the differences in ground vegetation are most striking. Within a few yards this can change from bracken to rushes, to bog myrtle, to bell heather and heath, sometimes as irregular patches in a matrix of moorland grasses. It is to these plant associations that we owe the variety of colour found on the hillsides where the land is used for sheep grazing, colours that change with the seasons of the year from the russets of the brackens in autumn to the warm purple of the heather hillsides in August.

From the start of creating forests in this locality the forester has been aware of the need to devote considerable care and attention to "landscape" the plantations into the countryside. Virtually all the remnants of the oak woods acquired with the land have been retained. These can be seen at Rowardennan, Aberfoyle and Achray, all being on the lower ground in the valleys or by lochsides. On the more visible hillsides rising from these the planted tree species are varied and related to the previous ground vegetation. Larch was planted where there was bracken, Scots or Lodgepole pine where there was heather and Norway or Sitka spruce where there was grass or rushes. Further colour variation was achieved by adding small areas of Douglas or Silver firs and by retaining the birch, alder, rowans and willow which survived in the steep-sided burns. By following the former ground vegetation patterns a degree of irregularity was achieved on the slopes which mask the higher proportions of pure spruce plantations in the "dead ground" behind.

Rising from the rounded tops of the oakwoods through the more pointed tops of the variety of coniferous species, the top edges of the forest received the same sympathetic consideration in that to maintain variety and contrast, to give interest to the eye, the top edge leaves smooth clear horizons next to parts where the forest is carried over the top. Where planting stops part way up a hillside the top boundary is carried up into hollows and down round rocky outcrops to enhance natural features. Alongside the Dukes' Road from Aberfoyle to the Trossachs the plantations were kept well back from the road to retain the magnificent views.

ENJOYING THE OUTDOORS

Long before the Forestry Commission was created this locality was popular as a tourist and recreation region, and since its first acquisition the Commission has had this public requirement in mind. In 1953, Coronation Year, the Forestry Commission declared its land holding the "Queen Elizabeth Forest Park" thereby granting the public access to it. Control of wild life, being exercised by the Forest Rangers only for the protection of the forests and adjoining land-use interests, has the effect of creating an extensive park within which a wide range of wild life, including birds of prey, can breed and where the visitor can walk without fear of disturbing game shooting.

Being within an hour's drive of most of the major urban area of the central lowlands of Scotland, most of those who come are day visitors seeking a few hours away from the clamours of urban life. Others are on tour or on holiday and spend a night or a week in the locality. Other parties come from schools, youth organisations

54

or colleges, and may be seeking physical recreation or pursuing educational studies. For all these many varied requirements the Forestry Commission endeavours to make provision and the chapter on "General Information" in this guide lists much that is available. With such high public usage a degree of control must be exercised to ensure that, by pursuing their own requirements, one visitor does not inadvertently disturb anothers enjoyment. Pony trekkers ride over roads used the following day by a car rally, ornithologists or geologists study without disturbance in an area used for orienteering competitions next day, boys and girls on Duke of Edinburgh Award Scheme or sponsored walks may be active only a short distance away from a military exercise, all unaware of each others' presence and firm in the belief that they have the place to themselves. Forests can absorb tremendous numbers of people if all uses are well organised in advance.

The Forestry Commissioners have drawn up by-laws which apply to this Forest Park as well as to all their other forests, to both protect the forests and to enable the visit to be an enjoyable one. An over-riding rule is that cars and motor cycles are not allowed into the forest unless specially authorised, as there must be some places where people can get away from traffic. Since this guide was first published in 1954 there have been substantial changes both in forest practices and in the requirements from forests. It is quite likely that this edition will equally be overtaken by events and the visitor is thus welcome to discuss any aspect with Forestry Commission staff.

* * *

Jock, when ye hae naething else to do, ye may be ay sticking in a tree; it will be growing, Jock, when ye're sleeping.

—Scott, *Guy Mannering*

Yet live there still who can remember well,
 How, when a mountain chief his bugle blew,
Both field and forest, dingle, cliff, and dell,
 And solitary heath, the signal knew;
And fast the faithful clan around him drew.
 What time the warning note was keenly wound,
What time aloft their kindred banner flew,
 While clamorous war-pipes yell'd the gathering sound.

—Scott, *The Lady of the Lake.*

FOLK LORE

By Lord Bannerman

Loch Ard, meaning the "high loch", is the central feature of this, the wildest and perhaps most beautiful Forest Park in Britain. Its western boundary is the heather-clad hill land topped by Ben Lomond (the mountain of the beacon), descending steeply to form the "Bonnie Banks". North and east the Park stretches almost to Loch Katrine and to the hill lands around Aberfoyle, thus taking in a goodly portion of the famed tourist area of the Trossachs.

The legendary figure of Rob Roy once trod the glens and passes of this magnificent region. Just south of the boundary of the park on Loch Lomondside is the Pass of Balmaha, through which the cattle reived from the lush valleys of the Leven and Endrick were taken by this wild chieftain, outwitting his enemies by driving them on a hidden sandbank shallow through Loch Lomond from Ross Priory

56

Plate 38.   The view west over Loch Achray towards Ben Venue.

Plate 39.   Ben A'an, seen from the south across the still waters of Loch Achray.

Plate 40. The fishing station on Loch Venachar, looking south towards plantations near the Duke's Road.

Plate 41. Looking over Loch Achray towards the Trossachs Hotel.

Plate 42. The ruined Kirk of Aberfoyle. The gateway is flanked by cast iron mort-safes, designed to protect corpses from body-snatchers.

Plate 43. The Old Trossachs Church, by Loch Achray, with snow-clad Ben Venue rising beyond.

Plate 44. Beside the Black Water near Brig o' Turk; sunlit shallows below the alders.

Plate 45. Feeding the waterfowl on Loch Ard, close to Aberfoyle.

Plate 46.　Oakwoods along the Loch Katrine road, in the heart of the Trossachs.

Plate 47.　A car park and picnic point on the Duke's Road, beside Loch Achray.

Plate 48.   The Menteith Hills, clad in woods of pine, spruce and larch, rise above the
Forest Workers' hamlet of Braval, close to Aberfoyle.

Plate 49.   The Conic Hills near Balmaha, clad in conifer woods, are a remarkable feature
of the Highland Boundary Fault.

Plate 50. Sunset over Loch Ard, looking towards Ben Lomond.

to Balmaha. Rob Roy's Prison, by the side of the loch at the foot of Ben Lomond, is traditionally associated with a cape of rock falling sheer into the loch. There, it is said, Rob Roy held under duress any vassal whom he wished to punish. The story goes that he suspended one man who owed him rent, by a rope into an unscalable declivity of the rock, saying that although he was lowered in by the shoulders it would be by the neck that he would come out if the rent were not forthcoming!

The area of the Park two centuries ago was peopled mainly by crofters whose small black cattle, sheep and hill ponies roamed the hills, keeping down the bracken which has now covered most of the fertile valleys and hill sides.

Throughout the Park can be seen the remains of these crofting townships, usually marked by crumbling stone dykes. Often the mountain ash or rowan tree—to be seen today—guards these "larachs" or sites of the old croft-house, having been planted to ward off evil spirits. Superstition of this kind was rife amongst these communities, and some of the place names such as Creag a Bhocain, or the "rock of the ghost", close to Inversnaid, reflect the belief in the supernatural. From this region, as from many districts in the Highlands, the crofters were banished to make room for sheep and deer. Today the farming interests of the loch-side and Park are in the main confined to black-face sheep, and to a lesser extent hill cattle of the Highland or cross-Highland types.

Large sheep farms replaced the crofter husbandry. Now, in the main, trees are taking the place of sheep because of the encroachment of bracken and the difficulties of drainage of the hill lands. Inaccessibility is also a factor adverse to hill sheep farming. As a whole, the land has so deteriorated that a long-term rotation under timber has become the only economic utilisation possible. According to the *Statistical Account* of 1793 the main crops grown by the farmers and crofters were barley and oats, and these of course on the loch sides and in the valleys. "The highest cultivable land is 490 feet". The barley was used in the various "stills" of the period—some authorised, others, especially in later years, outside Government sanction. The Teapot Inn on the main road from Aberfoyle to Inversnaid owed both its name and its popularity to the travellers' need for a "Tea Pot" of the illicit brew of the countryside.

The whole area is described in the *Statistical Account* as being wet but healthy. In the parish of Buchanan, stretching to Inversnaid, the people are described as living to 70 or 80 years, "some reach 85 or 86 and there is one living at present who is 99". This old man was described as hale in every faculty, and after early breakfast setting out on long walks.

Such woodlands as were native to the region were mainly scrub birch and oak, and the condition of the latter seems to bear out the statistical record which tells how the children were kept away from school to peel the oak bark used for tanning, dyeing and other purposes. Forest covered most of the area in ancient times, and there must have been large trees in many parts of the Park. In the Duchray section of the Park it is said that in 1795 there was an alder tree near the Water of Duchray which measured "19½ feet round the trunk".

Aberfoyle is the biggest township in the Park, and is a thriving tourist centre through which flows the River Forth, which has its source on the north side of Ben Lomond.

The Park area will reward any visitor whose wish it is to view a world-famous highland area of Scotland. But the enquiring visitor will find that history has its pages still to be read in the physical evidences of the terrain—ranging from the old lime kilns of the crofters near the peat banks fuel reserve—to the resting place of saints marked by ancient monument and "cashels". Especially will the study of the place names and their meanings usher the visitor into an enchanting world of historical significance. This is a countryside that will delight both eye and mind.

*   *   *

Oh! here's a cup to my friends and my darling own place!
Glad am I that by fortune my mother she bore me here.
It might have been far on the plains of the Saxon stranger,
With never a hill like Dunchuach or Duntorvil near,
And never a fir with its tassels to toss in the wind,
Salt Fyne of the fish before, and Creag Dubh of the deer behind!

—Neil Munro, *Home.*

GAELIC PLACE NAMES
AND THEIR DERIVATIONS

Assistance with the translation of the Gaelic place names was given for the first edition by Mr. A. Nicholson, M.A. This has been checked for the second edition by Mr. J. M. Beaton, Forester, Achray Forest.

Direct translations are not always practical because Gaelic, being a live language, has developed different dialects over the years. This leaves any list open to challenge by differing opinions.

ABERFOYLE	*Obair-phuill,* i.e. *abar* (estuary) of muddy stream or pool
ALLT CLACH AN LAOIGH	Burn of the stone of the calves (pasture)
ARNDRUM	*Druim fhearn,* alder ridge
BAD DEARG	Red clump
BALLEICH	*Baile an eich,* township of the horses
BALMAHA	Seat of St. Tatha, i.e. *Baile mo Thatha*

59

BEINN A BHAN	*Beinn a' Bhain*, in mod. Gaelic, "fan" (flat), i.e. ben of the flat top
BEINN AN FHOGARAIDH	Ben of the driving (of the wanderer, or of the fugitive from justice)
BEINN BHREAC	Mottled ben
BEINN UIRD	Mount of the rock mass: *Ord* is a hammer-like mass of rock
BEN DEARG	Red mountain
BEN LEDI	Mountain of gentle slope: *Beinn an leothaid*
BEN LOMOND	Mountain of the beacon, i.e. *lumen*
BEN VENUE	*A' bheinn mheanbh*, hill of the young cattle
BLAIRHULLICHAN	Flat of the little mound, i.e. *Blar an Tullachain*. *Tullach*=rounded hill rock
BLAIRVOCKIE	Flat of the bogie: *Blar a' Bhogaidh* locative of *bogach*, old gen. *bogaidh*
BLARUSKINBEG	Flat of the streamlet: *Blar an Uisgein Bhig*
BRAEVAL	*Bhaile:* The brae of the township
BRIG O' TURK	*Prochaid an Tuirc*, i.e. Bridge of the boar
BUCHANAN	*Both a' Chamain*, the canon's seat (booth)
CAILNESS	*Coill Innis*, Wood of the recess. Protected area among mountains
CAISTEAL CORRACH	Pointed castle—Point=*corrag, corran*
CAMUS AN LOSGAINN	Nook or cove of the toads
CAORUNN ACHAIDH BURN	*Achadh a' Chaoruinn*, field of rowans
COILLE MHOR HILL	Great wood hill
COIRE EIRIGH	Hollow of the ascent
CORRIE	*Coire*, cauldron, usually a hollow, with water in bottom, in mountain area
CORRIEGRENNAN	*Coire a' ghrianain*. Grianan was a sunny knoll, often, in past, a burial place because sun on it most of day
COULIGARTEN	*Cul a' ghartain*. Nook of little cultivated patch, in moorland
CRAIGMORE	Great rock, i.e. *Creag Mhor*
CREAG A BHOCAIN	Rock of the ghost or goblin
CREAG AN CAORACH	*Creag nan Caorach*. Rock of the sheep
CROIT AN SHLUIC	*Croit ant-sluic*. Croft of the hollow
CRUACHAN	The heap. *Cruach*+diminutive affix, *an*
CRUINN A BHEINN	*Cruinn Bheinn*. Round mountain
DRUM OF CLASHMORE	*Druim na Claise Moire*. Ridge of the great rift
DRYMEN	*An Druimean*. The little ridge
DUBH LOCHAN	Black lochan

60

DUCHRAY	Black sheiling
DUN DHAMH	Rounded hill of the stags
DUN NAM MUC	Rounded hill of the pigs
EASTER SALLOCHY	Eastern farmstead of the willows — *Seileach*
EILEAN GORM	Green isle
FRENICH	*Raineach.* Place of bracken (often with prothetic "f")
GARBEG HILL	*An Garbh Beag.* The little rocky height
GARTLOANING	*Gart an Lonain.* Cultivated part of the boggy flat
GARTMORE	*An Gart Mor.* The large field
GLEANN GAOITHE	*Gleann na Gaoithe.* Glen of the winds
GLEANN MEADHONACH	Mid Glen
GLEANN RIABHACH	Brindled glen
GUALANN	Shoulder ridge
INNIS ARD	High pasture (*Innis*, originally island protected by water, transferred to sheltered place among hills)
INVERSNAID	*An-t' Snathad* (The needle), name of stream + *Inbher* (estuary)
KELTY WATER	Wooded place, from *Coilltidh*
KINLOCHARD	*Ceann an Loch Aird.* Head of high loch
LAGAN AMAIR WOOD	*Amar* (vat); a narrow ravine, i.e. *lagan* (little hollow) of the ravine (*Lagan an Amair*)
LAKE OF MENTEITH	Lake of the moorland of the Teith
LOCH ACHRAY	Loch of the level field
LOCH ARD	High loch
LOCH ARKLET	Loch of the bend of the slope
LOCH CHON	Loch of the dogs
LOCH DRUNKIE	Loch of the "ridge of the back"
LOCH DUBH	Black loch
LOCH KATRINE	*Loch Caitriona*, girl's name
LOCH LOMOND	From Ben Lomond: *see* above
LOCH VENACHAR	Old Gaelic, *Benn* (pointed). The pointed loch
LOCHAN MAOIL DHUINNE	Lochan of the brown tonsured one, i.e. priest
LOCHAN MHAIM NAN CARN	Lochan of the mound of the cairn
LOCHAN SPLING	(Derivation unknown)
LON MOR	Great boggy flat
MAOL AN TAILLIR	Brow (hillside) of the tailor
MAOL RUADH	Ruddy brow, i.e. upland

MAOL AN LARUIRNE	Little brow of Lorn. Modern, *Maol an Lathurna*
MEALL EAR	East lump
MENTEITH HILLS	"Moorland of the Teith" Hills
MULAN A T'SAGART	Mound of the priest
PTARMIGAN	Named after bird (cf. Glen Lyon. *Meall an Tarmachain.* Letter "p" an interloper here)
RENAGOUR	*Ruighe nan Gobhar.* Ridge of the goats
ROWARDENNAN	*Rudha Aird Eanain.* Point of the height of Adamnan, i.e. Biographer of St. St. Columba (*Eanan* is from *Adhamhan,* little Adam)
ROWCHOISH	*Rudha a' Chois.* Point of the hollow
RUDHA FUAR A CHAS	*Rudha Fuar a' Chois.* Cold point of the steep hollow
SRON AONAICH	Neb or nose, i.e. ridge, of the slope
SRON LOCHIE	Neb of the place of lochs
STRATHCASHELL POINT	*Strath a' Chaislighe.* Ford across river (cf. *Caislighe* of *Glen Lyon,* from *Cas+slighe*)
STRONMACNAIR	*Stron mhic an aidhir.* Neb of son of sallow one; from *odhar*
STUC A BHUIC	Peak of the buck
TROSSACHS	*Na trasdaichean.* Obsolete word meaning transverse glen, joining two others. cf. Welsh *traws*

*　　*　　*

With heels to valley, sun on face,
Stones slowing down the eager pace,
The heather clutching at the knees
And sweat more cool than cooling breeze,
Go upwards, onwards to the light
Of snow that keeps the granite bright.

—William Jeffrey, *Nevis.*

HILL WALKS

By Douglas Scott and Roger Hurst

WITHIN the Forest Park there is a whole range of possible walks, ranging in severity from the extremes of the high mountain tops through the gentler hill slopes to the sheltered loch sides. The visitor is advised to select those walks or parts of walks which are best suited to his particular requirement or degree of experience. Visitors may walk over any of the forest roads within the Forest Park and this facility is offered as an opportunity to walk on roads free of busy traffic and noise. If you come by car or motor cycle please park your vehicle so that it does not cause an obstruction and so that it will not be damaged by other visitor's vehicles. Follow the Country Code and, please, take your litter home.

Many walking routes through the Queen Elizabeth Forest Park are marked by a series of coloured discs which indicate the destination. The key to these colours is as follows:—

Rowardennan	*Red*	Aberfoyle	*Yellow*
Inversnaid	*White*	Kinlochard	*Blue*
Drymen	*Brown*	Brig o' Turk	*Green*
Gartmore	*Orange*	Callander	*Black*

The outstanding feature of the Park from the walker's point of view is the splendid position on the edge of the Highlands. A complete gradation of country can be experienced when approaching from the south or east, from the softer cultivated land to the alpine crags of Ben Lomond. The Park contains two of the most popular and well-known mountains in Scotland, Ben Lomond and Ben Venue. Rugged little hills abound, set with lochs like gems among their natural woods. The area includes the greater part of some of the very finest cross-country routes in the Highlands.

There is no single centre for exploration, but there are instead a number of good bases on the boundaries. There are camp sites at Rowardennan and Aberfoyle, and Youth Hostels at Rowardennan, Kinlochard and Trossachs (Lendrick). Numerous hotels are available throughout the area, and limited accommodation can often be obtained from kindly people in cottages and farms.

When setting off for an excursion among the hills it is always advisable to carry a few essentials, including a one-inch map and a compass even on the path up Ben Lomond. Attention to clothing is equally important. Boots should be strong and some kind of wind-proof jacket or anorak is advisable. In winter, conditions on the tops can be severe, even when the sun shines on a windless day in the glens. Then extra woollen clothing should be carried and a balaclava and gloves. An ice axe or a good stick can be a great help.

The varied interest of these hills and the general absence of big rock faces (other than Ben Lomond, parts of Ben Venue, Ben A'an and Craigmore) makes this an ideal district in which to learn the important elements of hill-craft, rather than among the cliffs and gullies of mountains such as those around Glen Coe. When mistakes are made in these early stages of mastering the techniques there is a greater margin of safety.

From the wide choice of possible walks within the Park, a selection of nine are described in some detail below. The mileages given are only approximate. Many an argument has raged in camp and bothy over the difference between miles on the map and miles on the ground. Time should be allowed for twists and turns and the extra distance of ups and downs, difficult to estimate on the flat map, as well as for bad weather. The suggested times are average and might easily be halved or doubled.

1. ROWARDENNAN TO INVERSNAID ON LOCH LOMONDSIDE (8 miles – 3 hours)
From the pier car park take the road running north past the youth hostel. Just before the entrance to Ptarmigan Lodge a new forest road has been constructed and though this is above the public

footpath it is easier to follow. It was probably along this path that Rob Roy's sons James and Robert carried off the young widow Jean Key in December 1750 (see chapter on History). Just south of Rowchoish a short spur road cuts off to the left. Follow this down to the lochside and then resume the route of the public footpath on your right which leads you to the William Ferris Memorial Shelter at Rowchoish. This building, the last of a hamlet which in 1759 totalled nine families, was restored by the Scottish Rights of Way Society and opened by Prof. Sir Robert Greive. Proceeding north the plantations are left by a stile over the deer fence, and shortly after the walker leaves the Forest Park, crossing a foot bridge at Cailness Farm. The path leads to Inversnaid, crossing a beautiful waterfall by a bridge at the Hotel. During the summer months the Loch Lomond steamer "Maid of the Loch" calls at Inversnaid. Inversnaid is at the end of the public road from Aberfoyle and Stronachlachar.

2. ASCENT OF BEN LOMOND 3,192 (3½ miles – 3 hours up)

Ben Lomond is the only mountain in the Forest Park over 3,000 feet and the most southerly in Scotland over that height. It is a mountain of character and those who only know the broad-shouldered aspect from Strath Endrick or the south shores of Loch Lomond could hardly guess at the fine crags of the northern corries. Owing to its isolated position the view from the summit is one of the finest in Scotland. The whaleback of Ben Nevis is plainly seen among the wild tangle of mountains to the west and north. In the east are the Ochils and Stirling with its dark castle-crag. While southward lies the smoke veil of the Clyde towns among their low hills, and beyond them rise the peaks of Arran. The path to the summit begins opposite the hotel at Rowardennan. The lower part ascends north-east between plantations planted in 1959 on the right and 1970 on the left, passing out of the top fence at 1,000 feet above sea level. Before climbing into the ridge above the Halfway Well the watershed on the right leads over to Kinlochard and Aberfoyle in the centre of the Forest Park. Ascending the steep climb over the Well by the broad south ridge, you have now achieved 1,800 feet above sea level, after which the direction is more or less north. In summer it is easy to follow and marked by cairns, but the last thousand feet are steeper, with the final stretch running along the narrow summit crest. The steep cliffs and gullies of the north face, often snow lined until the early summer, are now seen. In early spring the summit is often like an alpine peak with great snow-cornices jutting over the edges. The steep cliffs and gullies are best avoided by all but experienced mountaineers.

65

3. THE OLD GARTMORE ROAD: DRYMEN TO ABERFOYLE
(10 miles – 4 hours)

From Drymen go north over the quiet moorland road through the older Garadhban woods devastated by the January 1968 gale but since replanted, and out onto the crest of the hills where a small fishing lochan on your left lies between young trees planted in 1970 and 1971. Descending the hill, the Forest Park boundary is skirted affording wide views across Flanders Moss at the head of the Forth Valley to the Lake of Menteith. Take the left hand branch at the road junction at Dalmary, crossing the Kelty Water just before Chapelarroch, where Rob Roy lifted the Duke's Factor plus £300 rent money (see chapter on History). The Claggan Burn just before the village of Gartmore is the county boundary between Stirlingshire and Perthshire.

Three quarters of a mile after the attractive village of Gartmore, and just before Crinigart House, turn left into a forest road. After a short distance this is joined by another road from the left, after which it descends into the Gartloaning Valley. Over the burn the road crosses another and climbs up the hillside. Over the crest of the rise two more roads join on the left, leading to Easterhill Cottage, before which a left turn will put you in the direction for Aberfoyle.

4. PIPE TRACK ROAD TO KINLOCHARD AND ABERFOYLE
(10 miles – 4 hours; 15 miles – 6 hours to Aberfoyle)

Originally the Glasgow Corporation Water Works road and now the Lower Clyde Water Board road (known as the Pipe Track or Corporation Road). Leave the main Glasgow-Aberfoyle Road at Auchentroig Old Schoolhouse 1½ miles north of Ballat, by turning left and following the road through the young woodlands planted in 1962 known as the "Parks of Auchentroig". Crossing the Gartmore—Drymen Old Road the Corporation Road passes the Corrie Forestry houses and the entrance to Corrie Farm, and winds up over the ridges of the Highland Fault line to drop down on the Bell House at the Duchray Water. Here there is a choice of either crossing the Duchray water by the Water Board's Bridge, which will take you over the ridge to Kinlochard, or turning left on the forest road just before the Bell House and thereafter taking a right hand turn. Passing below Blairvaich, cross the Duchray Water by a bridge over a steepsided gorge, and turning right at the T-junction. Both routes rejoin after passing under the stone aqueduct at a crossroads where the downhill road leads to Kinlochard. This lies five miles west of Aberfoyle, which is easily reached along a good tarred road; alternatively, take path 6 (page 68) in reverse.

5. ABERFOYLE TO ROWARDENNAN
(12 miles – 5 hours)

Cross the Forth at Aberfoyle, passing the old roofless Kirk with two mortsafes flanking the door, and crossing the Pow Burn, make for the manse where Sir Walter Scott wrote one of his novels. Bear right for Balleich and after passing several forest workers houses the forest is entered by a tarmacadam road, which is a long-term experimental surfacing trial, to determine the relative costs of different surfacing materials. Passing two forest roads branching off to the left and off to the right, the Bofrishlie Burn is crossed by a concrete bridge and its valley is now followed through the Forest. Three more forest roads branch off on the right before the same burn is recrossed by a second bridge (during this next length the "Long Walk" of Loch Ard Forest crosses this walking route and great care is needed not to take that in error). After the bridge, ignore the first road branching off on the right, and at the next cross roads bear right; so far you have been following the "Telephone Road" which is the main spinal road of the forest from which, as you will have seen, many other feeder roads branch off. From now on you are on a link road called the "Clashmore Ford" which joins the "Corporation Road" referred to in the notes of Path No. 4 above. Bearing right on the Corporation Road it follows the line of the Loch Katrine aqueduct. Just before the Bell House, fork off to the left and follow this road, taking the first right, passing another house called Blairvaich, after which the Duchray Water is crossed by a wooden bridge high above the Black Linn Falls in the rocky gorge below.

At the next T-junction turn left, departing from path No. 4, and follow this road past the entrance to Corriegrennan Farm on the left, after which the next feature is the stone aqueduct, also on the left, carrying the second of the Lower Clyde Water Board's aqueducts over the Duchray Water. Half a mile further on take the left hand fork, recross the Duchray Water and start to ascend the Lomond Ridge with the Bruach Caoruinn Burn on your left.

By the time you have reached the wide turn-round point at the end of the forest road, you have attained an altitude of 1,000 feet above sea level. Keeping the burn on your left for a while, follow the path until you reach the stile over the Deer Fence as you leave the plantations.

Travelling almost due west you cross an undulating area of deep peat bogs to join up with the Ben Lomond path (No. 2 above), just at the foot of the ridge below the Half-way Well. Follow this path down to the left to Rowardennan. If time and energy permit, the ascent of Ben Lomond can be made by turning right when Path 2 is reached.

6. ABERFOYLE TO KINLOCHARD
(6 miles – 2 hours)

Leave the centre of the village by the Stronachlachar (Inversnaid road) and after one mile bear left at Milton. Over the river bear right and enter the forest past Smithycroft, turning right again to gain the very attractive lochside road past Loch End cottage, which is on the banks of Little Loch Ard.

A couple of hundred yards farther on there is a choice, either follow the low road, or bear left and take the high road which rejoins the lower road eventually. The low road has close intimate views of the loch whereas the high road enjoys sweeping views over the whole loch, and its surroundings.

After skirting the water for the last time the road climbs through the fields to a T-junction with the Corporation road above Couligarten house. Turning right this road leads down to the village of Kinlochard.

7. ABERFOYLE TO BRIG O'TURK
(6 miles – 2 hours)

Ascend the Duke's Road past the David Marshall Lodge to gain the flat stretch known as the County Flats. Hill Cottage, the house on the left, marks the entrance to the Slate Quarries which were once a major source of employment for Aberfoyle.

Gaining the top of the Duke's Road the views change from Aberfoyle and the Forth Valley to long views down the valley over Loch Venachar to Callander, across to Ben Ledi, into Glen Finglas. After passing the surprising and unexpected view of Loch Drunkie on the right you should leave the Duke's Road by striking off on the path to the right. But before taking this, a brief diversion up the hillside to the left will gain the Tom an t-Seallaidh (viewpoint) from which even wider views of Ben A'an, Loch Katrine and Ben Venue can be seen.

Entering the forest after leaving the Duke's Road, the path descends through the forest, emerging past Achray Farm over Brig o'Michael to the public road. The Trossachs are to the left and Brig o' Turk hamlet and Lendrick Youth Hostel to the right.

8. BEN VENUE, 2,392 FEET
(3 miles – 2½ hours by the path)

This route to Ben Venue starts from Ledard on the north side of Loch Ard. A well marked path, running north, follows the side of the Ledard burn to the gap east of 'Beinn Bhreac' 2,295 feet. It then contours the north slopes of Creag Tharsuinn, working eastward to the west ridge of Ben Venue.

The approaches to Ben Venue *from the south* are long and gradual and the summit appears to consist of two small tops rising slightly above the level of the surrounding ridges.

Seen from the north or from the east across Loch Achray it has the appearance of a real mountain, rising steeply above the rough woods of the Trossachs. Two fine approaches from this side start at the Achray Hotel, entering the forest at the rear of the Hotel, and following the forest road to the first fork.

The easiest route is to take the left-hand fork and follow the route by the burn in Gleann Riabhach to the head of the glen, where, after crossing the Deer Fence, you can scale the edge of the wide corrie to the Ben Venue ridge.

The most arduous route is to take the right fork until you leave the forest by the gate in the deer fence, at the Sluices on the outlet from Loch Katrine. Then climb the ridge above in a south-westerly direction, making zig-zags to avoid rocky outcrops to gain the south shoulder. Traverse the east top, which is only a few feet below the main summit. Although there are no cliffs of much interest to the rock climber, there are many little crags where care is needed, especially if mist or bad weather should develop.

The view from Ben Venue is much less extensive than that from Ben Lomond, but as it also rises near the southern lowlands the eye can range far down the estuaries of the Forth and Clyde. Its greatest charm however is in the near views of lochs and wooded shores stretching away to north and east.

9. BEN A'AN

(2 miles – 1½ hours)

Leaving the public road two hundred yards on the Loch Katrine or west side of the Trossachs Hotel, a steep path climbs up through the young plantations, suddenly opening out on to the open hill with the sharp peak of Ben A'an above. This path is very steep but the views from any part of it, over Loch Katrine and Loch Achray, are all enjoyable.

There are steep and dangerous rock faces to Ben A'an and considerable caution is necessary as these are only for the expert well equipped climber.

The owner of Duchray Castle requests that we inform the visitor that the castle, its gardens and grounds are private property and not in any way part of the Queen Elizabeth Forest Park, which is entirely restricted to Forestry Commission property

"Oh, lassie, wilt thou gang,
Tae the Lomond wi' me,
The wild thyme's in bloom,
An' the flower's on the lea?
Wilt thou gang, my dearest love?
I will ever constant prove
I'll range each hill and grove
On the Lomond wi' thee.

* * *

The hynd shall forsake
On the mountain, the doe;
The stream o' the fountain
Shall cease for tae flow;
Benlomond shall bend
His high brow tae the sea
Ere I tak' tae my bower
Any flower, love, but thee."

THE TROSSACHS IN LITERATURE

By Herbert L. Edlin

These lines from *Amang the Lomond Braes* by Robert Tannahill, the weaver-poet of Paisley, aptly express the mood in which most holiday-makers would wish to approach the magnificent Trossachs countryside today. Ben Lomond itself, visible from afar across the Central Lowlands, is one of Scotland's best-known landmarks, while the road up the western shore of Loch Lomond, being one of the principal gateways to the Highlands, has been trodden by generations of travellers. Dr. Johnson was here in 1773 during his tour of the Hebrides with Boswell, who recorded:

"After breakfast, Dr. Johnson and I were furnished with a boat, and sailed about upon Lochlomond, and landed on some of the islands which are interspersed. He was much pleased with the scene."

The next notable literary visitor was William Wordsworth, who, as a young man of thirty-three, came here in 1803 with his sister Dorothy. The latter has left us an intimate record of their travels in her *Journals*, under the heading *Recollections of a Tour made in Scotland*. Accompanied by the poet Coleridge, the Wordsworths left Dumbarton on August 24th, and travelled in their one-horse car to Luss and Tarbert. They crossed Loch Lomond by boat, landed at Inversnaid, and walked to Glen Gyle at the head of Loch Katrine. Here Wordsworth was given to understand that Rob Roy lay buried (though his grave is actually in the kirkyard of Balquhidder, many miles away), and it was in this belief that he penned a long poem entitled *Rob Roy's Grave*, which is now remembered chiefly for the lines:

". . . . . the good old rule,
Sufficeth them, the simple plan,
That they should take who have the power,
And they should keep who can."

On the following day, August 27th, the Wordsworths travelled by boat right down Loch Katrine to the Trossachs, where they landed and walked for a time, admiring the views of Ben Venue and Loch Achray, which Dorothy described as follows:

"After we had landed, we walked along the road to the uppermost of the huts, where Coleridge was standing. From the door of this hut we saw Benvenue opposite to us—a high mountain, but clouds concealed its top; its side, rising directly from the lake, is covered with birch trees to a great height, and seamed with innumerable channels of torrents . . . .
Above and below us, to the right and to the left, were rocks, knolls, and hills, which, wherever anything could grow—and that was everywhere between the rocks—were covered with trees and heather; the trees did not in any place grow so thick as an ordinary wood; yet I think there was never a bare space of twenty yards: it was more like a natural forest where trees grow in groups or singly, not hiding the surface of the ground, which, instead of being green and mossy, was of the richest purple. The heather was indeed the most luxuriant I ever saw; it was so tall that a child of ten years old struggling through it would often have been buried head and shoulders, and the exquisite beauty of the colour, near or at a distance, seen under the trees, is not to be conceived . . . .

71

At the opening of the pass we climbed up a low eminence, and had an unexpected prospect suddenly before us—another lake, small compared with Loch Ketterine, though perhaps four miles long, but the misty air concealed the end of it. The transition from the solitary wildness of Loch Ketterine and the narrow valley or pass to this scene was very delightful: it was a gentle place, with lovely open bays, one small island, corn fields, woods, and a group of cottages. This vale seemed to have been made to be a tributary to the comforts of man, Loch Ketterine for the lonely delight of Nature, and kind spirits delighting in beauty. The sky was grey and heavy,—floating mists on the hill-sides, which softened the objects, and where we lost sight of the lake it appeared so near to the sky that they almost touched one another, giving a visionary beauty to the prospect. . . . This small lake is called Loch Achray."

The party then returned up the loch in pouring rain, to lodge at the ferryman's house. The next day they walked back, again through heavy rain, to Inversnaid, where they encountered the girl to whom Wordsworth later addressed his famous poem *To a Highland Girl*, which opens:

> "*Sweet Highland girl, a very shower*
> *Of Beauty is thy earthly dower!*
> *Twice seven consenting years have shed*
> *Their utmost beauty on thy head:*
> *And these grey rocks; this household lawn;*
> *These trees, a veil just half withdrawn;*
> *This fall of water, that doth make*
> *A murmur near the silent Lake;*
> *This little Bay, a quiet road*
> *That holds in shelter thy abode;*
> *In truth ye do together seem*
> *Like something fashion'd in a dream.*"

After crossing the ferry, Coleridge returned to England, but the Wordsworths continued their tour into the West Highlands, returning by way of Callander. On September 11th they again approached the Trossachs, travelling along the shores of Loch Venachar to the head of Loch Achray; here the road ceased, and they sent their car back to Callander in charge of a boy. They continued their way on foot through the Trossachs and up the north side of Loch Katrine, to the ferryman's house, where they stayed the night. Next day they went on to Inversnaid, crossed the ferry, turned north, and walked nine miles into Glen Falloch; then, accompanied by a guide, they crossed the river and went south-eastwards over the trackless hills to Glen Gyle and down to the head of Loch Katrine, where they were met by a boat which took them on to their starting point. This round tour must have involved over twenty miles of walking, and four miles by boat.

72

Plate 51. Planting a young spruce on a slice of turf thrown up by a forest plough.

Plate 52. An airplane scatters a phosphatic fertiliser to speed the growth of a young plantation.

Plate 54. The second cut from the opposite side removes support and the tree falls.

Plate 53. Felling a larch with a power saw; the first step is cutting the "sink".

Plate 56. Deep in the wood, the chokerman, who secures the haul-in cable to the logs, signals to the winchman, telling him when to haul in.

Plate 55. A tractor-powered winch draws a bunch of logs to the roadside, ready for loading.

Plate 57. Using his power saw, a tree feller trims away branchwood from a felled conifer; the tape measure fixed to his belt simplifies length measurements for cross-cutting.

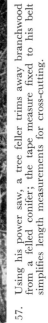

Plate 58   A hydraulic grab quickly loads the trimmed logs on to a lorry.

Plate 59. Cock ptarmigan in late spring, with the change from winter white to summer brown plumage almost complete.

Plate 60. Pintail drake.

Plate 61. Red squirrel climbing a Scots pine trunk.

Plate 62. Billy goat, one of the wild herd that roams Ben Lomond.

Plate 63. Golden eagle and eaglet at their eyrie; note how tough heather stems have been used to build the nest.

Plate 64. Red deer stags.

Plate 65.   Wild cat.

Plate 66.   Blackcock displaying at the lek, or mating ground.

Nevertheless, the Wordsworths were off early next morning, again with a guide, and this time they went northwards from Loch Katrine and over the hills to the headwaters of Loch Voil. They passed the ancient burying place of the MacGregors, and went down the lochside to Balquhidder, reaching Strathyre before nightfall. Here, fatigued after a tramp of nearly twenty miles, they lodged for the night. But they were up early next morning, and before eight o'clock had walked the nine miles to Callander, where they stopped for breakfast. Here they resumed their horse-drawn car, and by nightfall they had passed through Stirling and reached Falkirk. Considering that they were in unfamiliar country, which at that time had only the roughest of roads and tracks, and that they had often to contend with inclement weather and difficulties in securing accommodation, their daily itineraries are remarkable.

Wordsworth's poems were not completed until he had returned to Westmorland, but the source of their inspiration is clear. On the high pass between Loch Katrine and Loch Voil, Dorothy tells us: "William here conceived the notion of writing an ode upon the affecting subject of those relics of human society found in that grand and solitary region." Further on, as they descended into the strath, she notes "It was harvest time, and the fields were quietly—might I be allowed to say pensively?—enlivened by small companies of reapers. It is not uncommon in the more lonely parts of the Highlands to see a single person so employed." The outcome was that famous lyric *The Solitary Reaper*, so lovely that it must be quoted in its entirety:

> *"Behold her single in the field,*
> *Yon solitary Highland Lass,*
> *Reaping and singing by herself—*
> *Stop here, or gently pass.*
> *Alone she cuts and binds the grain,*
> *And sings a melancholy strain.*
> *Oh! listen for the Vale profound*
> *Is overflowing with the sound.*

> *No nightingale did ever chaunt*
> *So sweetly to reposing bands*
> *Of travellers in some shady haunt*
> *Among Arabian Sands;*
> *No sweeter voice was ever heard*
> *In spring-time from the cuckoo-bird*
> *Breaking the silence of the seas*
> *Among the farthest Hebrides.*

> *Will no one tell me what she sings?*
> *Perhaps the plaintive numbers flow*
> *For old unhappy far-off things,*
> *And battles long ago;—*
> *Or is it some more humble lay—*
> *Familiar matter of to-day—*
> *Some natural sorrow, loss, or pain*
> *That has been, and may be again?*
>
> *Whate'er the theme, the Maiden sung*
> *As if her song could have no ending;*
> *I saw her singing at her work,*
> *And o'er the sickle bending;*
> *I listen'd till I had my fill,*
> *And as I mounted up the hill*
> *The music in my heart I bore*
> *Long after it was heard no more."*

Whereas the Wordsworths recorded their impressions of contemporary Highland life and scenery, Sir Walter Scott's attention was fixed on the past. His *Lady of the Lake,* first published in 1810, is a long romantic poem relating the legendary adventures of a mediaeval Scottish king and his court, who set out from Stirling Castle to hunt the deer in the wild forests of the Trossachs, and of their encounters with the Highlanders. The modern reader may find its long narrative passages, in octosyllabic couplets, tedious, and consider the "songs" with which they are interspersed an unduly artificial device.

But, on its first appearance, which coincided with the dawn of the "romantic age" of nineteenth century literature, it gained immediate popularity; and ever since the constant stream of tourists coming to visit the scenes that it made famous have been an impressive witness to the magic of Scott's pen. The high-lights of the poem are its descriptions of the countryside wherein the action is set. Scott, of course, knew the ground intimately; he first visited the district as a young legal apprentice in 1790, and in later years stayed at the Manse of Aberfoyle, where the room in which he worked may still be seen. He travelled on horseback over the course of the journeys made by certain of his characters, to satisfy himself that these were feasible in the time that the action of the poem required. Perhaps the finest passage is that describing the stag hunt, with which the main action of the poem opens, and from which the following examples are taken:

> *"The stag at eve had drunk his fill,*
> *Where danced the moon on Monan's rill,*
> *And deep his midnight lair had made*
> *In lone Glenartney's hazel shade.*

* * *

The noble stag was pausing now,
Upon the mountain's southern brow,
Where broad extended, far beneath,
The varied realms of fair Menteith.
With anxious eye he wander'd o'er
Mountain and meadow, moss and moor,
And ponder'd refuge from his toil,
By fair Lochard or Aberfoyle.
But nearer was the copsewood grey,
That waved and wept on Loch-Achray,
And mingled with the pine-trees blue
On the bold cliffs of Benvenue.
Fresh vigour with the hope return'd,
With flying foot the heath he spurn'd
Held westward with unwearied race,
And left behind the panting chase.

* * *

Few were the stragglers, following far,
That reached the lake of Vennachar;
And when the Brigg of Turk was won,
The headmost horseman rode alone."

Contrasting with the idealised romanticism of mediaeval chase and tourney, featured in this early poem. Scott's later novel *Rob Roy*, published in 1818, gives a much more faithful picture of real life in this outlying corner of the Highlands. His long preface, which well deserves study, shows that he was dealing with characters not far removed from his own times; less than a generation separated him from the freebooters who descended from the fastness of Glen Gyle to plunder the fat cattle from the Lennox valleys, and drive them north through such routes as the Bealach nam Bo—the pass of the cattle—beside Loch Katrine. He records indeed, that on occasion the raiders might seize a bride as well! Comparatively little of the action of *Rob Roy* takes place in the Trossachs neighbourhood; but the encounter, at the Clachan of Aberfoyle, between Rob Roy and that worthy Glasgow citizen Baillie Nicol Jarvie, is memorable both for creation of atmosphere, and for the skilful delineation of contrasting Scottish characters, Highland and Lowland.

Rob Roy himself, who figures in our frontispiece and chapter heading, was a farmer, cattle drover and leader, freebooter, and leader of irregular forces, who flourished between the years 1660 and 1734. He was the son of Lt. Col. Donald MacGregor of Glengyle, while his mother was a Campbell. History records that he led a cattle reiving at Kippen in 1691, farmed Craigroyston near Cailness at the north-east end of Loch Lomond between 1701 and 1715, took part in the Jacobite rising of 1715, and eventually settled at the farm of Kirkton in Balquhidder, He was engaged in the various feuds and political intrigues of the Dukes of Argyll, Atholl and Montrose, and for a period after 1715 was outlawed, narrowly escaping, after capture, on two occasions. The "Garrison" or barracks built by the Government near Inversnaid, to keep in check the unruly Macgregors, may still be seen; it was twice taken by surprise by clansmen, the soldiers disarmed, and the building destroyed.

Though many legends, and much history, are associated with this wild clan country so romantically situated where the Highlands fringe the Lowlands, few traditional songs—either Gaelic or Scots—have originated here. Yet one—the *Bonnie Banks of Loch Lomond*—has gone round the world. Little is known of its source, though it is believed to be connected with the Jacobite rising in 1745. There are several versions of the words, one of which may fittingly end this chapter:

> *"Oh! ye'll tak' the high road and I'll tak' the low road*
> *An' I'll be in Scotland before ye;*
> *But wae is my heart until we meet again*
> *On the bonnie, bonnie banks o' Loch Lomon'."*

* * *

76

O to mount again where erest I haunted
Where the old red hills are bird-enchanted,
And the low green meadows
Bright with sward,
And when even dies, the million-tinted,
And the night has come, and planets glinted,
Lo, the valley hollow
Lamp-bestarr'd!

—Robert Louis Stevenson, *In the Highlands*.

GENERAL INFORMATION

THE information given here is to assist you in planning your visit to the area, whether your stay is a short one or of longer duration. Space available limits the detail which can be given and perhaps this is as well for the situation is never static and always subject to change and variation. The sources of information are given to enable the visitor to check that these facilities are still available or to ascertain what is new on the scene.

TOURIST BOARDS

The Scottish Tourist Board, Rutland Place, Edinburgh, 1, supplies excellent information covering the whole of Scotland which will enable you to plan your holiday to include a visit to this and other Forest Parks. They will also provide the addresses of the local tourist associations.

Callander and District Tourist Association, 2 Ancaster Square, Callander, covers the central and eastern parts of the Forest Park.

It maintains Information Offices at Callander and Aberfoyle, produces an accommodation list, and will also supply details of all the facilities available in the locality.

There are also Tourist Information Offices at Stirling and Glasgow.

MAPS

Ordnance Survey one-inch-to-the-mile Tourist Map "Loch Lomond and the Trossachs" (HMSO, 50p); also Sheet 53, *Loch Lomond*, for western portion; and Sheet 54, *Stirling*, for eastern portion (HMSO, 40p per sheet).

Bartholomew's half-inch-to-the-mile series: Sheet 48, *Perthshire*, for northern portion; Sheet 44, *Firth of Clyde*, for south-west; Sheet 45, *Mid-Scotland*, for south-east.

ACCESS TO THE PARK

Since the first edition of the guide was published much of the local public transport has been withdrawn, and the situation may well change during the period of this second edition.

BUS SERVICES

The visitor is advised to obtain details from Messrs. W. Alexander & Sons Ltd., Head Office, Brown Street, Camelon, Falkirk, as services vary between winter and summer, and between days of the week. The main routes are listed below, but only the two Aberfoyle services actually enter the Park. See Location Map.

Drymen to Glasgow	Callander to Edinburgh
Drymen to Balloch	Callander to Stirling
Aberfoyle to Glasgow	Callander to Oban
Aberfoyle to Stirling	

RAIL SERVICES

Nearest rail accesses are Stirling (16 miles), Glasgow (25 miles), and Balloch (14 miles). From Balloch Pier British Rail also operate the *Maid of the Loch* steamer service on Loch Lomond, during the summer months only.

At Stirling British Rail have a Motorail Terminus, for cars from the south.

AIRPORTS

Glasgow: Glasgow Airport, Abbotsinch, Paisley (distant 25 miles); Edinburgh: Edinburgh Airport, Turnhouse, Edinburgh, 12 (distant 50 miles).

Many hotels operate their own transport service for their patrons. There are facilities for car hire, taxi service, private bus parties, etc.

Access routes for the walker, cyclist and private motorist are not listed as they generally prefer to determine their own routes from the maps available.

Of the ferry services shown on the older map editions, many have been either discontinued or become an irregular service which can only be checked by local enquiry.

NOTE: VEHICLES, EXCEPT THOSE AUTHORISED FOR FORESTRY OR FARMING, ARE NOT PERMITTED ON FOREST ROADS.

ACCOMMODATION

The most useful information is to be obtained from the Accommodation Lists of the local Tourist Associations, the usual Guides published by motoring and other associations, etc. There is a fairly full range of Hotels, Bed and Breakfast Houses, Restaurants, Cafes, Inns, Bars, etc., fairly well distributed throughout the area. Centres under which accommodation is listed include: Aberfoyle, the Trossachs, Callander, Drymen, Gartmore and Rowardennan.

CAMPING AND CARAVAN SITES

There are numerous sites around the Park area which are listed in the usual guides. Within the Forest Park the Forestry Commission offers the following facilities:—

CASHEL (Rowardennan): A delightful site on the eastern shore of Loch Lomond with direct access to the loch.

COBLELAND (Aberfoyle): Another most attractive site by the River Forth with direct access for walking in the adjoining forest, or to use as a base camp for exploring the Park.

Both these public camping sites have resident wardens who welcome the visitor and are available to assist wherever possible. They maintain the services of their sites to a high standard and provide camp shop facilities.

Details of the moderate charges, which vary from time to time, are shown in the pamphlet *Forestry Commission Camping and Caravan Sites*, post free from the District Office, Forestry Commission, Aberfoyle, Stirling. (As a guide, the rates in 1973 were 20p per person per night; children aged 5-15, 10p; subject to an addition for Value Added Tax.)

On a minimum facility basis the Forestry Commission also provide a series of Youth Camp Sites scattered throughout the Forest Park. These are available to Youth Organisations on advance

79

booking. Application should be made to District Officer, Forestry Commission, Aberfoyle, Stirling.

NOTE: NO CAMPING OR OVERNIGHT PARKING IS PERMITTED WITHIN THE FOREST PARK OTHER THAN AT THE ABOVE SITES.

YOUTH HOSTELS

The Scottish Youth Hostel Association have the following hostels within the Park area:—

Rowardennan Youth Hostel, Rowardennan, Drymen, Glasgow; telephone Balmaha 259.

Loch Ard Youth Hostel, Kinlochard, Stirling; telephone Kinlochard 216.

Lendrick Youth Hostel, Brig o' Turk, Callander; telephone Trossachs 227.

A degree of advance planning and booking at these and other neighbouring hostels can permit a very full exploration of the locality, or the study of a project, e.g. geology, geography, ornithology, historical, etc., etc.

OUTDOOR RECREATION

FISHING

A very full range of freshwater angling is available in and around the Forest Park. To obtain access to these fishings the following list will be of assistance:—

Loch Lomond	Loch Lomond Angling Improvement Association.
Loch Ard Loch Chon	⎱ The Aberfoyle Angling Protection ⎰ Association.
Loch Venacher River Blackwater	⎫ Callander Town Council, via Messrs. ⎬ James Bayne, Fishing Tackle Shop, ⎭ Callander.
Loch Achray Loch Drunkie	⎫ Forestry Commission, via Aberfoyle ⎬ Office, The David Marshall Lodge, ⎭ or the Post Office, Brig o' Turk.
Lochan Spling Lochan Ghleannain Lochan Reoidhte River Forth Duchray Water	⎫ ⎪ Telephone Recreation Club and Civil ⎬ Service Sports Council, via The ⎪ Newsagents, Aberfoyle. ⎭
River Forth	Mr. D. Galpin, via Mr. E. Billet, Glenwood, Gartmore.
Lake of Menteith	The Proprietor, Lake Hotel, Port of Menteith, Stirling.

80

Loch Katrine ⎫ The Lower Clyde Water Board, 419
Loch Arklet ⎬ Balmore Road, Glasgow, N.2.
Glen Finlas Reservoir ⎭

LOCH STEAMERS AND BOAT TRIPS

Loch Katrine: *Sir Walter Scott:* Summer Service: Trossachs Pier to Stronachlachar, operated by Lower Clyde Water Board, 419 Balmore Road, Glasgow, N.2.

Loch Lomond: *The Maid of the Loch:* Summer Service: Balloch Pier, Balmaha, Rowardennan, Tarbert, Inversnaid, Ardlui, operated by British Rail.

Balmaha and Rowardennan: Boat trips are available on Loch Lomond.

PONY TREKKING

Several operators offer ponies at centres throughout the Park area for trekking, staging or general riding. Addresses are available from Tourist Offices and advertisements in the hotels, etc. This Forest Park is a major pony trekking area in Scotland and operators range from two or three ponies to sixty or more.

SAILING

Most clubs offer day facilities for visitors, though because numbers are limited advance enquiries are advised:—

Loch Venachar: The Secretary, Loch Venachar Sailing Club, Callander, Perthshire.

Loch Achray: The Trossachs Hotel and the Loch Achray Hotel, Trossachs, Callander, Perthshire.

Loch Ard: The Secretary, Loch Ard Sailing Club, c/o Honeyman, Jack and Robertson, 13 Allan Park, Stirling.

Loch Lomond: Numerous clubs and organisations.

CANOEING

Loch Venachar: The Secretary, Venachar Canoe Club, Callander.

Loch Lomond: The Clyde Canoe Club, Blair, Balmaha, Glasgow.

ORIENTEERING

Events are arranged by several clubs. Details from the Honorary Secretary, Scottish Orienteering Association. (92 Coillesdene Avenue, Edinburgh, EH15 2LG).

GOLF: BOWLING GREENS: TENNIS COURTS

Facilities are available at Aberfoyle, Drymen and Callander.

CLAY PIGEON SHOOTING

Events are held at Aberfoyle. Details from the Secretary, Loch Ard Gun Club.

There are no organised facilities in the locality, but bathing is permitted in most of the lochs, though the visitor is advised to enquire locally for the best and safest places.

NOTE: BATHING IS NOT PERMITTED IN LOCH ARKLET, LOCH KATRINE, GLEN FINLAS RESERVOIR OR ANY WATERS FEEDING THESE WATER SUPPLIES.

WALKING

See chapter on "Hill Walks".

FOREST TRAILS

The "Sallochy Forest Trail" at Rowardennan on Loch Lomond-side provides a good introduction to the forests and the enjoyment that can be derived from leaving your car in the car park and rediscovering your feet.

PHOTOGRAPHY

The Forest Park set in this superb scenery provides excellent opportunities for many types of photographic studies.

NOTE: WILD LIFE PHOTOGRAPHY IS NOT PERMITTED WITHIN THE FOREST PARK WITHOUT A FORESTRY COMMISSION PERMIT.

NATURE CONSERVANCY

An excellent Nature Trail and other facilities are provided on the island of Inchcailloch, off Balmaha, Loch Lomond. Access is by boat from Balmaha, and details can be obtained from Nature Conservancy, The Castle, Loch Lomond Park, Balloch, Dunbartonshire.

DEPARTMENT OF THE ENVIRONMENT

On the Lake of Menteith, just outside the Forest Park, a motor boat leaves from the jetty by the Lake Hotel, to the Island of Inchmahome, the site of an ancient priory which was for a short time the home of Mary Queen of Scots. Details are displayed at the car park adjoining the jetty.

CAR PARKING AND PICNIC SITES

LOCH LOMOND

On the shores of the loch, alongside the road to Rowardennan and within the Forest Park, the Forestry Commission and Stirling County Council have jointly provided a series of car parks and picnic areas. The last one of these is the large car park at Rowardennan Pier, complete with toilets.

LOCH CHON

Where the public road meets the lochside just south of Frenich the Forestry Commission has provided a series of lay-bys and the shore line makes a very pleasant picnic area. It is at this point that the old General Wade Road to Inversnaid Garrison parts company with the public road and a pleasant walk is to follow this into the plantations as far as the old Wade Bridge where it crosses the first burn.

DUKE'S ROAD

Though the Forest Park runs to the edge of the road surface on either side, the Forestry Commission have kept the plantations back to retain the superb views and provide numerous parking spaces, picnic sites and play areas on either side. This is a very extensive area, being some five continuous miles on both sides of the road from the edge of the village of Aberfoyle to the old Toll House on the side of Loch Achray.

LOCH VENACHAR

Approximately half way along the northern shore, between the public road and the loch, Perthshire County Council have developed parking and picnic areas which are very popular with visitors.

NOTE: PLEASE TAKE YOUR LITTER HOME AND LEAVE THE SITE AS YOU WOULD LIKE TO FIND IT.

SPECIAL FACILITIES

These may be arranged within the Forest Park through the District Officer, Forestry Commission, Dunans, Aberfoyle, Stirling. Examples of such facilities are:—

Sponsored Walks and other similar events, Car Rallies, Group Visits, Barbecues, Specialist study requirements, etc.

DAVID MARSHALL LODGE

This superb picnic pavilion was gifted to the Forestry Commission by the Carnegie Trust in 1960. Situated on the hillside above the village of Aberfoyle, near the start of the Duke's Road to the Trossachs, it commands fine views of the central part of the Forest Park and the Forth Valley. It is named after a former Chairman of the Carnegie Trust.

The Resident Warden welcomes the visitor and is available to assist where possible. He is responsible for the maintenance of the same high standards as at the Camp Sites and provides a shop from which light refreshments can be obtained. Visitors are very welcome to take picnics on the premises; hot water is available.

The Lodge commands magnificent all-round views, each window presenting a different aspect. To the south-east across the flat Flanders Moss of the upper Forth Valley to the Fintry Hills; to the south-west over the village and the central part of the Forest Park to the mountainous ridge of hills which form the east bank of Loch Lomond; to the north-east the exquisitely landscaped forest ascending the Highland Fault lines of the Menteith Hills; to the west all 3,192 feet of Ben Lomond. Within each of these panoramic breathtaking views there is a wealth of detail of shapes, colours, and textures which draw the visitor back time and time again.

A long, low single-storey building, beautifully built in local stone, it commands the top of a rocky bracken- and birch-covered knoll against the backing of higher hills, the craggy heather-covered Craigmore on one side and the forested Menteith Hills on the other. A tarmacadam walk leads up to it from the two car parks (100 cars) which are left behind in a screen of birch and oakwoods. The building and its environs are completely unfenced which not only gives vast areas for picnicking but also a complete feeling of freedom and release from all urban constraints. Older people and the physically handicapped may drive up to the Lodge; all others must get away from their cars and walk the quarter mile to gain the top of the knoll. The views are hidden until suddenly revealed on reaching the Lodge.

For those who wish to walk, paths leave from the Lodge, one from the south wing into the forest and another a more arduous path to Craigmore.

Printed in Scotland for Her Majesty's Stationery Office by McCorquodale (Scotland) Ltd, Glasgow
Dd 131959 K128 5/73